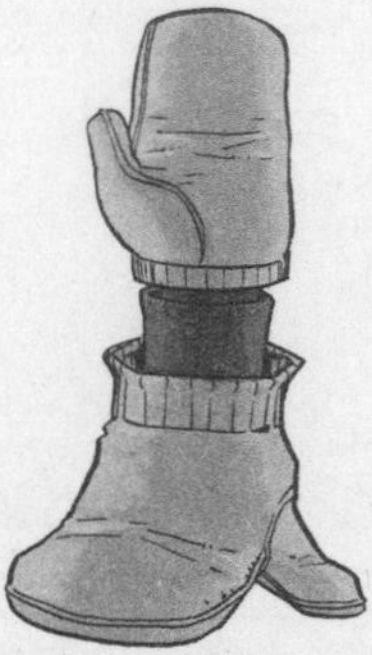

Thanks for purchasing volume 16!
It's getting cold, huh! I actually get excited about winter, because I love it!! COLD, though!!

KOHEI HORIKOSHI

MY HERO ACADEMIA

16

SHONEN JUMP Manga Edition

STORY & ART **KOHEI HORIKOSHI**

TRANSLATION & ENGLISH ADAPTATION **Caleb Cook**
TOUCH-UP ART & LETTERING **John Hunt**
DESIGNER **Julian [JR] Robinson**
SHONEN JUMP SERIES EDITOR **John Bae**
GRAPHIC NOVEL EDITOR **Mike Montesa**

Printed in the U.S.A.

Published by VIZ Media, LLC
P.O. Box 77010
San Francisco, CA 94107

10 9 8 7 6 5 4 3 2 1
First printing, December 2018

VIZ MEDIA
viz.com

ratings.viz.com RATED T TEEN

PARENTAL ADVISORY
MY HERO ACADEMIA is rated T for Teen and is recommended for ages 13 and up. This volume contains fantasy violence.

SHONEN JUMP
shonenjump.com

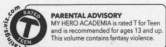

MY HERO ACADEMIA

KOHEI HORIKOSHI

SHONENJUMP MANGA

CHARACTERS

ALL MIGHT
SHOTA AIZAWA
TAMAKI AMAJIKI
IZUKU MIDORIYA
EIJIRO KIRISHIMA

STORY

One day, people began manifesting special abilities that came to be known as "Quirks," and before long, the world was full of superpowered humans. But with the advent of these exceptional individuals came an increase in crime, and governments alone were unable to deal with the situation. At the same time, others emerged to oppose the spread of evil! As if straight from the comic books, these heroes keep the peace and are even officially authorized to fight crime. Our story begins when a certain Quirkless boy and lifelong hero fan meets the world's number one hero, starting him on his path to becoming the greatest hero ever!

MY HERO ACADEMIA

Vol. 16

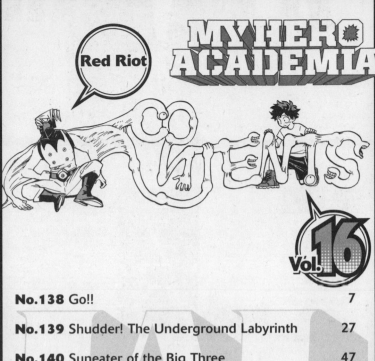

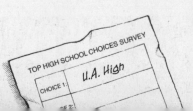

...WE LEARNED OF A SECRET UNDERGROUND FACILITY IN THE HASSAIKAI COMPOUND—AN AREA NOT IN THE PUBLIC RECORDS.

AND THE LITTLE GIRL WE WERE OUT TO SAVE WAS HIDDEN AWAY IN A ROOM DOWN THERE.

THANKS TO NIGHTEYE'S PEEK INTO THE FLUNKY'S FUTURE...

TMP

TMP

THIS WAS CRITICAL INFORMATION, GIVEN THE OTHERWISE DAUNTING PROSPECT OF SEARCHING THE ENTIRE COMPOUND.

STILL, THE ROUTE HE TOOK REPRESENTED THE QUICKEST PATH TO OUR GOAL.

...SO WE WEREN'T CLUED IN TO THE ENTIRE LAYOUT OF THE BASEMENT.

ON HIS WAY TO HER ROOM FROM THE UNDERGROUND ENTRANCE, THE MAN DIDN'T MAKE ANY STOPS OR DETOURS...

NO. 138 - GO!!

DRILL THEM INTO YOUR HEADS!

WE'VE GOT A LIST OF THESE HASSAIKAI PUNKS' REGISTERED QUIRKS. AS MANY AS WE COULD FIGURE OUT, ANYWAY.

ON THAT NOTE...

WE KNOW WHERE WE'RE HEADED, BUT IT COULD STILL BE A SLOG IF THEY'RE ANY GOOD WITH THEIR QUIRKS.

IT'S GREAT, KNOWING ALL THIS IS ADVANCE.

8:00 A.M.

IN FRONT OF THE POLICE STATION...

DON'T GIVE THEM TIME TO TAKE HER AWAY!

WE'RE HOPING TO CAPTURE EVERY LOWLIFE THERE...

...AS QUICKLY AS POSSIBLE!

RIGHT? PRETTY WEIRD.

FIRST IT'S DETECTIVE WORK, AND NOW A FULL-ON POLICE OPERATION...? SOMETHING NEW EVERY DAY.

Is that your pose?

I'M GETTING KINDA NERVOUS...

YOU'RE QUITE THE MORNING PERSON...

THEY AIN'T WASTING ANY TIME!

KLIK

KLIK

...GRAN TORINO'S NOT HERE...

HEY...

I WONDER WHY?

THE PROS ARE ALL SO CALM! I GUESS THEY'RE USED TO IT.

TRUE.

Mm...

SWIP

THEY DIDN'T TEACH US ABOUT THIS IN SCHOOL, SO I HAD A HARD TIME EARLY ON.

LET'S HOPE SO!

MAYBE HASSAIKAI AND THE LEAGUE'LL BOTH GO DOWN HARD TODAY.

IT'S NO GREAT LOSS.

HE WAS DISTRAUGHT NOT TO BE HERE, BUT WE'VE GOT PLENTY OF PEOPLE ALREADY.

I SEE...

HUH

...

IT TURNED OUT HE COULDN'T COME.

TSUKAUCHI LEARNED OF A BIG DEVELOPMENT IN THE LEAGUE OF VILLAINS CASE.

AI...RASER HEAD!

HEY!

ALL RIGHT...!!

YOU REMEMBER WHY I'M STICKING AROUND THE NIGHTEYE AGENCY SQUAD, RIGHT?
YEAH ...!
HEROES.
THEY'RE PROBABLY GONNA PUT UP A FIGHT, Y'KNOW.
SO IF YOU SPOT ANY ONE OF THEM RESISTING OR TRYING ANYTHING FUNNY...
I'M COUNTING ON YOU GUYS TO DEAL WITH IT!
HERE, TAMAKI. EAT SOME MARLIN.
WHY MARLIN?
FINE. I'LL TAKE IT.

WE'RE UP AGAINST A MAFIA GROUP THAT'S SOMEHOW SURVIVED UNTIL NOW...
...SO DON'T LET YOUR GUARDS DOWN FOR A SECOND. GET IN THERE...
...AND DO WHAT YOU'VE GOTTA DO!
MOVE OUT!

SHIE HASSAIKAI COMPOUND
WHOOO
SH

BOSS... SORRY, POPS.
IT'S ABOUT TO GET NOISY IN HERE.

8:30 A.M.
TIME TO ACT!!
ONCE I READ OFF THE WARRANT, THINGS ARE GONNA START MOVING!
LET'S TRY TO END THIS QUICKLY.

Tch!
YEAH, YEAH, WE GET IT. YOU DON'T TRUST US.
KEEP FOCUSED, ROCK LOCK.
'SNOT WHAT HE MEANT. STOP BEING SUCH A JERK.
HMPH!
WE YAKUZA HAVE ALWAYS LURKED IN THE SHADOWS, HIDDEN AWAY.
BUT DON'T EXPECT US TO FLINCH JUST CUZ THE POLICE AND SOME HEROES ARE OUT TO GET US!

WHAT'S GOING ON?

!!
CRASH!
IT'S KINDA EARLY FOR SO MANY GUESTS...
HELP THEM!

SH
UP
SK
ARE YOU OKAY ?!
YEAH... I'M GOOD.
THANKS. GET BACK IN THERE... QUICKLY.
JUST STAY HERE AND DON'T MOVE, OKAY?

WHOA, WHOA, WHOA! HOLD UP!!
THEY'RE ALREADY ONTO US!!
SO WHAT? LET'S JUST PIN HIM DOWN!!
YOU'VE GOT ME ALL WORKED UP...
OHHHH MAN...
BULGE
BULGE
GET BACK!!
WHAT DO YOU PEOPLE WANT?!

SHF SHF SHF
FOR NOW...
THERE'S NO SENSE IN SPLITTING UP THE GROUP ANY MORE THAN WE HAVE TO!
THE RYUKYU AGENCY WILL DEAL WITH THIS ONE...
...SO GO AND FINISH THIS JOB!
GRAB!!

SLAM
GO NOW!
LET'S HELP OUT!
RIGHT!
YOU HEARD THE LADY. GET IN THERE. GO, GO!!
ZOOSH
TSUYU! URARAKA! GIVE HIM HELL!
CATCH YOU GUYS LATER!!

YOU AIN'T WELCOME HERE, GET IT?!

THE HECK'S GOING ON HERE?

THIS POLICE GUY'S GOT GUTS. WOW...!!

WE'RE THE POLICE AND HEROES!

YOU'RE SUSPECTED OF THE PRODUCTION AND SALE OF ILLEGAL SUBSTANCES, SO WE'VE GOT A WARRANT TO SEARCH THIS PLACE!

COME QUIETLY, NOW!

WHAM

SLASH

QUIRK: LEAFIPULATION!!

FWIK

LIKE WE GIVE A CRAP!!

THE BIG GUY AND NOW THEM... ARE THEY NOT AFRAID OF US AT ALL?

TOMP
TOMP
TOMP
TOMP
KEEP MOVING!
STRAIGHT TO THE TARGET!!
THE WHOLE LOT OF THEM ARE MOVING IN SYNC AT FULL SPEED.
THEY KNOW EXACTLY WHERE THEY'RE GOING. SO PROBABLY...
...OUR OPERATION'S BLOWN. IF THEY FIND YOU, IT'S ALL OVER.
I FIGURED WE'D END UP HERE SOONER OR LATER...
JUST HAPPENED TO BE SOONER, I GUESS... THEY WON'T FIND ME, THOUGH.
"I WASN'T THERE.
THEY WENT WILD ALL ON THEIR OWN."

THAT'S HOW WE'LL PLAY THIS. THAT'S THE REASON I HAVE THESE PAWNS.
HA HA HA HA...
THEY'LL BUY US TIME.
WHEN CHISAKI CHOOSES SOMEONE TO WORK DIRECTLY UNDER HIM, HE MAKES THEM WEAR ONE OF THOSE MASKS, BECAUSE THEY'RE SURE TO BE DOING SOME REAL DIRTY DEEDS.
WHY THE MASKS? BECAUSE HE DOESN'T WANT TO BREATHE THE SAME AIR AS THOSE CONTAMINATED INDIVIDUALS... IT'S NOT ABOUT TRUST. JUST THEIR STATUS AS PAWNS.
THE EIGHT BULLETS OF THE HASSAI GROUP.

MEANWHILE, HIDE ERI AND EVERYTHING ELSE!
LEAVE NO TRACE BEHIND!

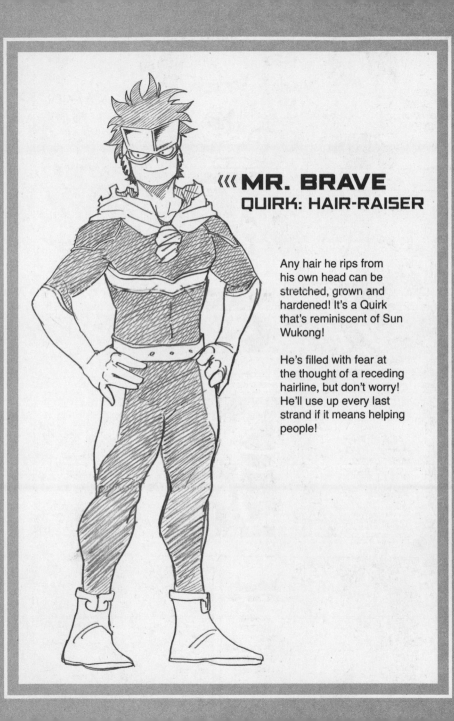

MR. BRAVE
QUIRK: HAIR-RAISER

Any hair he rips from his own head can be stretched, grown and hardened! It's a Quirk that's reminiscent of Sun Wukong!

He's filled with fear at the thought of a receding hairline, but don't worry! He'll use up every last strand if it means helping people!

HEY! WHAT'S THE BIG IDEA HERE?!
RAHHH
LIKE WE SAID, THIS IS A RAID!!

No. 139 - Shudder! The Underground Labyrinth

STAND DOWN!!
WHI?
BAM
CLEAR THE WAY!! IF YOU NEEDLESSLY FIGHT BACK, YOU'LL REGRET IT!!
THE GANG'S OUT IN FULL FORCE, JUST BUYING TIME...! SEEMS KINDA SELF-DESTRUCTIVE ...
EXCUSE US! WE'RE IN A HURRY HERE! SORRY FOR NOT TAKING OFF OUR SHOES!!
TOMP TOMP TOMP TO

NO. 139 - SHUDDER! THE UNDERGROUND LABYRINTH

BUT WE HAVE NO CHOICE... JUST GOTTA PUSH ON!

SOMETHING ABOUT ALL THIS DOESN'T FEEL RIGHT.

DON'T YOU THINK THIS FEELS KINDA SUSPICIOUS...?

BESIDES, IT'S COMMON KNOWLEDGE THAT THE MOB TENDS TO ACT WITH A REAL SENSE OF UNITY.

A LEAK? NAH. IF SO, THEY'D BE DOING A BETTER JOB OF DEALING WITH US.

MAYBE WE HAD A LEAK?

BUT IT SEEMED LIKE EVERYONE WAS PRETTY TRUSTWORTHY...

...MEANS THEY'RE PROBABLY USING THESE DISTRACTIONS TO CUT AND RUN.

ALL THIS PUSHBACK AND THE FACT THAT WE HAVEN'T SEEN CHISAKI OR HIS OFFICERS YET...

THE UNDERLINGS EXCHANGE SAKE CUPS AND PLEDGE LOYALTY TO THE BOSSES.

EVEN WITH THEIR FALL FROM GRACE, THESE GANGS HAVE ALWAYS EMPHASIZED LOYALTY ABOVE ALL ELSE.

NO DOUBT!!

LEAVING THE ROUGH STUFF TO YOUR FOLLOWERS WHILE MAKING A GETAWAY AIN'T MANLY AT ALL!!

LOYALTY? THAT'S A BUNCH OF CRAP!!

HERE.

WE JUST HAVE TO PRESS THESE PLANKS IN THE RIGHT ORDER.

SHP

SHP

THERE SHOULD BE A MECHANISM THAT OPENS UP THE WAY DOWN.

NOW WE JUST NEED TO WATCH OUT FOR UNFAMILIAR QUIRKS.

IF YOU HADN'T *SEEN* IT, THERE'S NO WAY WE'D KNOW WHERE TO GO.

RRMBBB

THIS IS LIKE SOME SORT OF NINJA HIDEOUT!

RRMBBB
KLIK
...!! BUBBLE GIRL!!
LIKE HELL YOU'RE GETTING PAST US!!

SHLIK
SHLIK
YOU TAKE ONE OF THEM!
BAM
QUIRK: CENTIPEDE ...
...CENTICOIL!!
GLARE
QUIRK: BUBBLE!
FWAH

CLAP!
SORRY, GUY!!
SHUP
SLAM
WE'LL MAKE SURE THESE THREE DON'T FOLLOW!
MY EYES!!
GO ON AHEAD. WE WON'T BE FAR BEHIND!
SO QUICK ...!!
LET'S MOVE !!

NOT MUCH FARTHER NOW!
TMP TMP TMP TMP TMP
!!
LOOKS LIKE A DEAD END!!
WHAT'S THE DEAL, NIGHTEYE?
THERE'S NO WAY THROUGH?!
FLIP
I'LL TAKE A LOOK!!
1000000

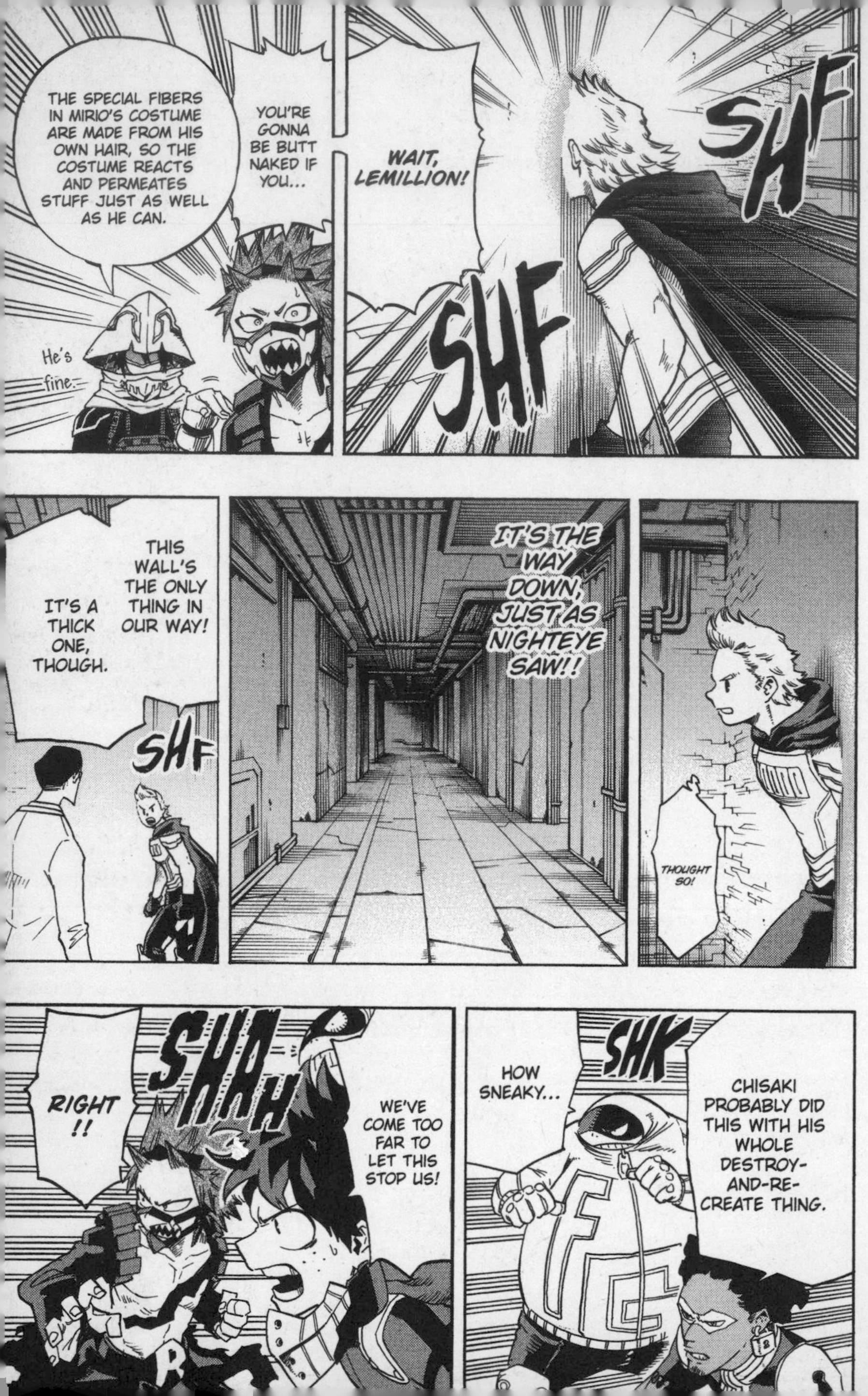
SHF
SHF
WAIT, LEMILLION!
YOU'RE GONNA BE BUTT NAKED IF YOU...
THE SPECIAL FIBERS IN MIRIO'S COSTUME ARE MADE FROM HIS OWN HAIR, SO THE COSTUME REACTS AND PERMEATES STUFF JUST AS WELL AS HE CAN.
He's fine.
THOUGHT SO!
IT'S THE WAY DOWN, JUST AS NIGHTEYE SAW!!
THIS WALL'S THE ONLY THING IN OUR WAY!
IT'S A THICK ONE, THOUGH.
SHF
SHK
CHISAKI PROBABLY DID THIS WITH HIS WHOLE DESTROY-AND-RE-CREATE THING.
HOW SNEAKY...
WE'VE COME TOO FAR TO LET THIS STOP US!
SHAH
RIGHT!!

THOUGHT YOU COULD SLOW US DOWN? WE'VE GOT NEWS FOR YOU, BUDDY!!
ONE FOR ALL
FULL COWLING
SHOOT STYLE !!

RED GUN
TURRET !!
THEY SMASHED THROUGH...
THESE KIDS GET THE JOB DONE, HUH...?
LET'S KEEP MOVING...
!!
THE CORRIDOR, IT'S...
SHF SHF
WAIT, LOOKIT THAT!!
SHF

SHF SHF SHF SHF

THE
HALLWAY!!
IT'S
TWISTING
AND
MORPHING!!

I'D SAY IT'S
GOTTA BE
THE HQ
DIRECTOR,
IRINAKA!

IT AIN'T
CHISAKI...
THIS ISN'T
HIS SHTICK!

SHF SHF SHF SHF

BUT THE
SCALE OF
WHAT HE'S
DOING HERE
IS OFF THE
CHARTS!

HE'S
SUPPOSEDLY
LIMITED TO
CONTROLLING
SOMETHING
THE SIZE OF A
FRIDGE...

BW

THAT'D
EXPLAIN
THIS...

MAYBE HE
GAVE
HIMSELF A
LITTLE
BOOST...

WHOOSH
ROLL
HIS QUIRK LETS HIM POSSESS OBJECTS AND CONTROL THEM FROM THE INSIDE...!!
MIMICRY!
HWOOOOO
HE MUST'VE TAKEN CONTROL OF THE CONCRETE IN THIS BASEMENT FACILITY...
...AND TURNED IT INTO A LIVING LABYRINTH!!
FWOOSH
I WAS ALL SET TO DEAL WITH SOME OBSTACLES, BUT THE WHOLE BASEMENT?
IT'S GOTTA BE TAKING A TOLL ON THE GUY'S STAMINA...
CAN YOU CANCEL IT OUT, ERASER?!
NOT UNLESS I CATCH SIGHT OF HIS REAL BODY...

WHAT'S OUR NEXT MOVE HERE? WE GOTTA BE QUICK... NO... IT'S HOPELESS...

MEANWHILE, THE BAD GUYS WILL HAVE ALL THE TIME IN THE WORLD TO ESCAPE.

SHFSHFSHF

THE PASSAGE-WAY KEEPS SHIFTING AROUND... WE'LL NEVER REACH THE TARGET AT THIS RATE.

TAMAKI!!

SHFSHFSHF

HOW CAN WE EVEN THINK ABOUT SAVING A GIRL WHEN WE'RE TOTALLY DOOMED?!

...!

YOU'RE SUNEATER, AFTER ALL!!

THIS ISN'T LIKE YOU!

I CAN MAKE IT!
PLUS!! WE CAN MAKE IT THROUGH THIS!
ALL THESE TWISTING HALLS DON'T MATTER AS LONG AS WE KNOW THE WAY TO THE TARGET.
ZOOSH
LEMILLION!
SENPAI!
FOOO
IT'S A RACE AGAINST THE CLOCK. THEY KNOW IT TOO. THIS IS ALL JUST TO BUY THEM TIME!
SH
SEE YOU GUYS ON THE OTHER SIDE!!
SHFF
MIRIO ...!!
SHEESH...!! WHAT'S WRONG WITH ME?!
LOOK AT MIRIO, GIVING IT HIS ALL LIKE THAT!!
IT'S CLEAR WHAT I'VE GOTTA DO.

...HE CAN'T PUT UP MUCH OF A FIGHT ON HIS OWN.

BUT, EVEN IF THE PUNK MAKES IT ALL THE WAY, THROUGH...

SHF

SHF SHF SHF

HE WALKED RIGHT THROUGH ME... NOT MUCH I CAN DO AGAINST THAT.

GINC

!

OOP

WE ONLY FELL ABOUT ONE STORY... THIS WASN'T MEANT TO KILL US...

SHLICK

THUD THUD THUD

UP THERE...

SHLICK

BUT...

IT'S ALL SEALED UP.

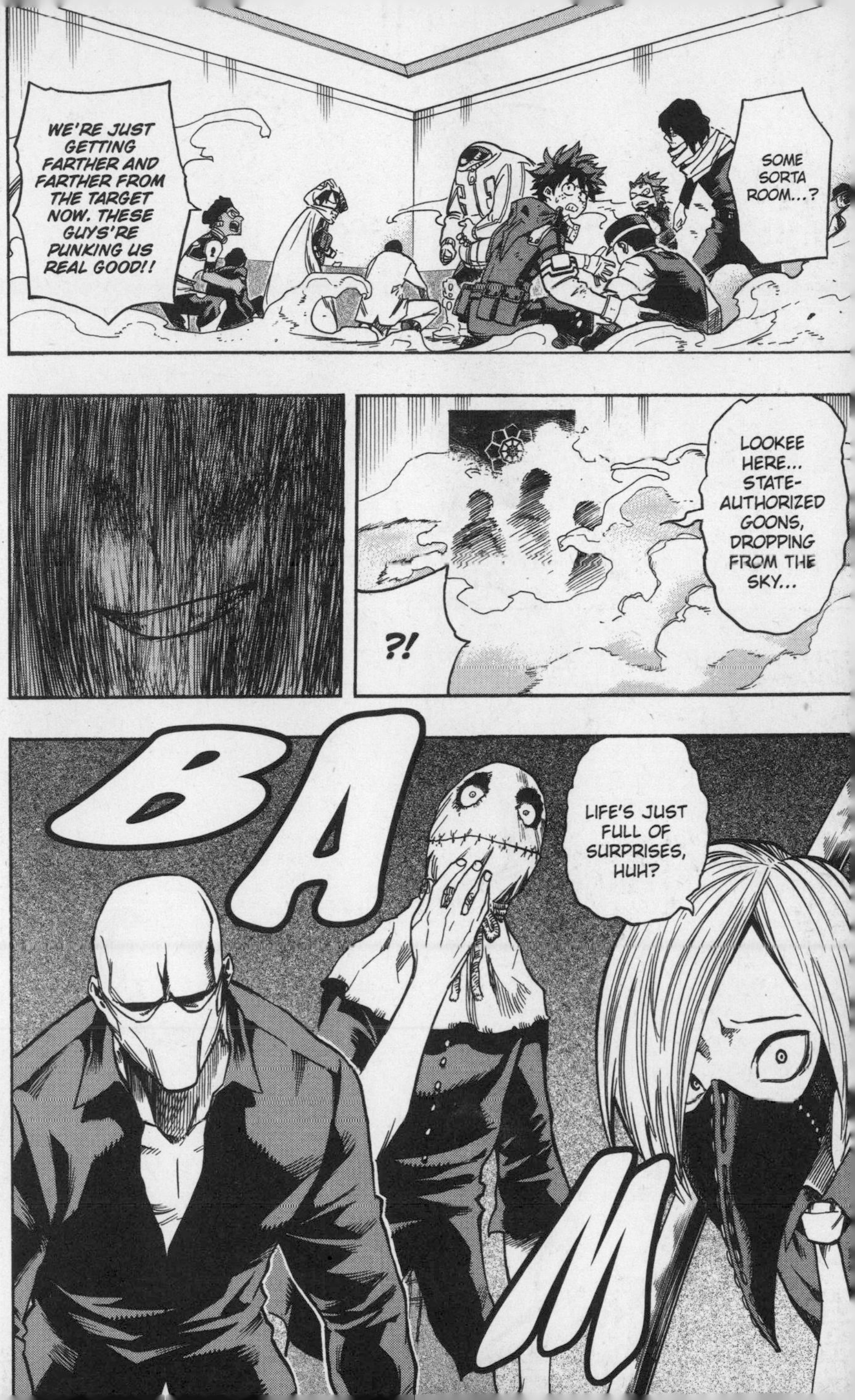
SOME SORTA ROOM...?
WE'RE JUST GETTING FARTHER AND FARTHER FROM THE TARGET NOW. THESE GUYS'RE PUNKING US REAL GOOD!!
LOOKEE HERE... STATE-AUTHORIZED GOONS, DROPPING FROM THE SKY...
?!
BAM
LIFE'S JUST FULL OF SURPRISES, HUH?

YOU PROS AND YOUR POWER...

...ARE ESSENTIAL TO THE MISSION! AS FOR THESE GUYS TRYING TO SLOW US DOWN...

SO THEY WANNA FIGHT...?!

HOW ABOUT WE SHOW 'EM WHAT US HERE PROS CAN DO...

...IS BECAUSE I'VE GOT YOU BY MY SIDE, TAMAKI.

IT'S NOT LIKE THAT AT ALL, MAN. THE REASON I WORK SO HARD...

...I CAN DEAL WITH THEM MYSELF!

THE COSTUME

MIRIO TOGATA'S COSTUME

LEMILLIOMET

He wears a helmet even though he can phase through things!!

It could come in handy during an unexpected battle, but it's likely to slip off sooner or later!

LEMILLIOSUIT

This costume's sole purpose is to stick with him when he phases.

The design is based on a costume worn by a hero from the past who saved and inspired Mirio.

TAMAKI AMAJIKI

I REALLY FLUBBED MY INTRO-DUCTION.

I'M... AMA...

I WANNA BE...A... HE...

THIRD GRADE. SPRING. I TRANSFERRED TO A NEW SCHOOL ON THE VERY FIRST DAY OF CLASSES.

NO. 140 - SUNEATER OF THE BIG THREE

AND IT'S NOT LIKE I'D BEEN ALL TOO SUCCESSFUL AT MAKING FRIENDS BEFORE EITHER.

I JUST THOUGHT OF MYSELF AS A PLAIN AND BORING GUY.

GAB   GAB

AS THE NEW KID WHO STARTED OFF ON THE WRONG FOOT, I DIDN'T HAVE THE GUTS TO ASSERT MYSELF WITH ANY OF THEM.

THE SEATING CHART HAD ALREADY BEEN MADE, AND EVERYONE WAS TOGETHER WITH THEIR CLOSE CLASSMATES.

THAT WAS WHEN YOU SHOWED UP...

AMAJIKI!! WHEN YOU SAID "HE" A MINUTE AGO...

...AND REACHED OUT TO ME.

YOU MEANT "HERO," RIGHT?! SO WHO'RE YOU A FAN OF?!

THE LEAD UNIT IS DOWN!
WHAT NOW?
WE GOTTA KEEP MOVING!!
GWOOM
THERE'RE MORE OF THEM THAN WE THOUGHT. BETTER START BY MOPPING UP THIS BUNCH...
No. 140 - Suneater of the Big Three
AS FOR THOSE GUYS TRYING TO SLOW US DOWN...
...I CAN DEAL WITH THEM MYSELF!
WHAT THE HECK, MAN?! LET'S DO THIS TO-GETHER!
YEAHHH! WORK TOGETHER, WHY DON'TCHA? MORE PIGS TO THE SLAUGHTER.
KSHING

THAT'S SETSUNO!! NOBODY PULL A GUN ON HIM!
HELP US OUT, HEROES!
I GUESS THE SECRET'S OUT! WHATEVER...
FWIP
IT'LL MAKE IT ALL THE EASIER...
...TO GO WILD ON Y'ALL!!
JMP
ZING
THAT WON'T WORK! NOW DROP THE BLADE!
MY QUIRK ...?!
A QUIRK CANCELER... LIKE ERI'S DEGRADATION QUIRK. I'VE HEARD ABOUT THIS BEFORE.
HE'S NOT A GUY YOU WANNA TANGLE WITH....
...BUT IT DOESN'T MATTER. WHAT WE'RE HERE TO DO IS TO...
...SLOW 'EM DOWN!
FWIP
NOTHING MORE...

BLADES 'N' BULLETS'LL JUST SINK INTO ME! COME QUIETLY IF YOU DON'T WANNA SUFFER!!
WE CAN USE OUR WEAPONS AS LONG AS ERASER'S DOING HIS THING! SURRENDER NOW!
THREATS LIKE THAT ONLY WORK ON PEOPLE WHO VALUE LIFE!
?!

"LARCENY" ... SETSUNO.
"CRYSTALLIZE" ... HOJO.
"FOOD"... TABE.

KLAK
I'LL TAKE YOU ALL ON!
I GET TO INDULGE IN PLENTY OF TAKOYAKI AT THE FAT AGENCY, SO MY OCTOPUS PROFICIENCY IS MAXED OUT...
...AND I'M PRETTY CAUTIOUS ABOUT THESE THINGS SINCE GETTING SHOT.
SNAP SNAP
KRRK KRRAK
FIGHTING THESE THREE DOESN'T SOLVE ANYTHING.
IF OUR PROS GET CAUGHT UP HANDLING THIS SITUATION, THEN WE'RE...
...PLAYING RIGHT INTO THEIR HANDS.
KRAK
HEH HEH HEH ...
G-GUH

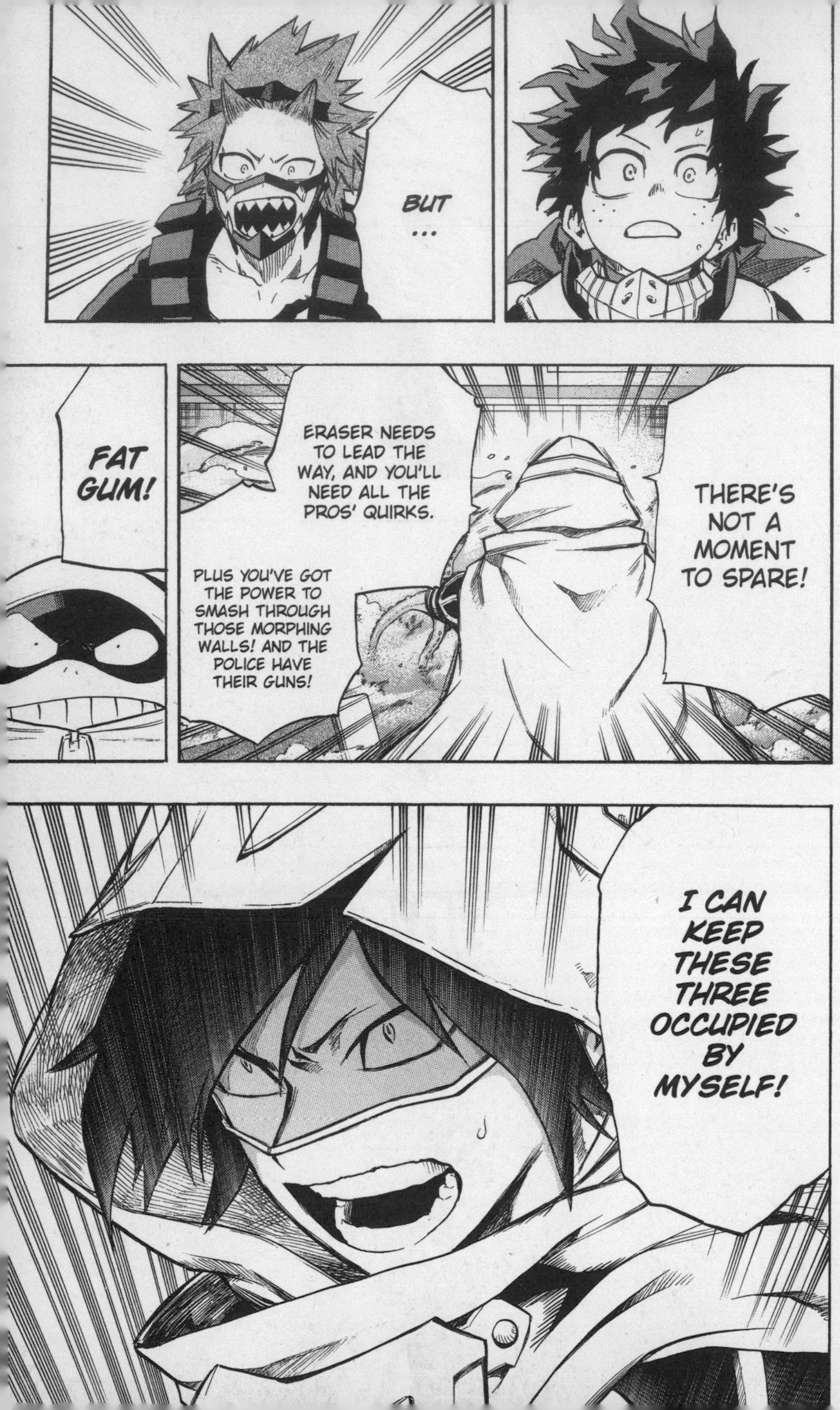
BUT ...
THERE'S NOT A MOMENT TO SPARE!
ERASER NEEDS TO LEAD THE WAY, AND YOU'LL NEED ALL THE PROS' QUIRKS.
PLUS YOU'VE GOT THE POWER TO SMASH THROUGH THOSE MORPHING WALLS! AND THE POLICE HAVE THEIR GUNS!
FAT GUM!
I CAN KEEP THESE THREE OCCUPIED BY MYSELF!

LET'S GO! THROUGH THAT DOOR!
FAT!
HEY, HEY, NOW. NOT SO FAST!
ZING
AGAIN ...?!
WHAP
I'LL KNOCK THEM OUT WHILE I'VE STILL GOT MY EYES ON THEM!

GO! NOW!!
HELP OUT MIRIO!
I JUST KNOW... HE'S GONNA TAKE THINGS TOO FAR AND NEED SAVING...

HE'S YOUR GUY, SO IT'S YOUR CALL, BUT IT SEEMS LIKE A BAD MOVE TO ME.

FAT!! WHAT'S THE DEAL, LEAVING HIM ALL ALONE BACK THERE?!

BUT DESPITE THAT, HE STILL ROSE UP TO BECOME ONE OF THE U.A.'S BIG THREE.

HE'S JUST LACKING SPIRIT.

THE PRESSURE HE PUTS ON HIMSELF TO BE PERFECT CRUSHES HIM.

HE'S MORE CAPABLE THAN ANYONE ELSE HERE.

SO IF HE SAYS HE'LL DEAL WITH THEM, I JUST HAFTA BELIEVE IN HIM.

I GUESS HE'S PRIORITIZING THE COPS UP ABOVE, BUT IT DOESN'T SEEM LIKE HE CAN MONITOR THE ENTIRE MAZE AND MOVE IT AROUND IN SUBTLE WAYS.

AND I'M NOT SEEING ANY TRACE OF IRINAKA OR HIS MIMICRY ABILITY DOWN HERE.

THIS TRIO'S HERE TO KEEP US FROM REACHING THE TARGET.

EITHER WAY, MY ROLE IS TO TAKE THESE THREE OUT OF THE EQUATION!

COULDN'T USE MY QUIRK AGAIN! THIS IS SERIOUSLY TOO FREAKY!

THAT ONE TALKS A BIG GAME... I SHOULD KNOCK THESE THREE OUT BEFORE ERASER'S ERASURE WEARS OFF...
SHK
SORRY, BUT YOU'RE ALL ABOUT TO TAKE A LITTLE NAP.
ZOOSH
!
KRI
SURPRISED? DID YA FLINCH? WE GET THAT YOU'RE IN A HURRY, BUT...
...YOU BETTER TAKE US MORE SERIOUSLY, Y'HEAR?
ESPECIALLY WHEN YOU'RE UP AGAINST THE LIKES OF US.

WHOK

THAT SNEAKY JERK'S QUIRK BOUGHT YOU SOME TIME, BUT THAT'S ALL IT DID.

WHOK

GUESS YA DIDN'T KNOW WHAT I WAS PACKING UNDER THIS HERE MASK...

GWGOOM

ZSH

TOMP

FWOOMP
KINDA HANDICAPPING YERSELF IF YA WON'T KILL US! WHAT A CHARMED LIFE YA MUST LIVE!
POP
LARCENY...
INSTANTLY STEALS A PERSON'S EQUIPMENT.
I GUESS MY SHELL COUNTS AS EQUIPMENT...?
WE'D GIVEN UP ON LIFE, Y'SEE!! WHEN WE TRIED TO KILL OURSELVES BY LEAPING TO OUR DEATHS...
...A HERO CAUGHT US! CAN YA IMAGINE OUR DESPAIR ?!
WE DIDN'T SEE THE POINT IN LIVING ANYMORE! THERE'S NO WAY YOU'D UNDERSTAND!

EVEN TRASH LIKE US HAVE PRIDE. WHEN GIVEN A JOB...YOU CAN BET WE'LL COME THROUGH!!

BUT THE YOUNG BOSS FOUND A NEW USE FOR OLD GARBAGE!

PEOPLE MAKE FINE USE OF THEIR QUIRKS AT ANY NUMBER OF JOBS. BEING A HERO'S NOT THE ONLY OPTION.
HOW WILL YOU BE USEFUL TO SOCIETY IN THE FUTURE? THAT'S WHAT WE'RE HERE TO EXPLORE IN QUIRK TRAINING.
FIZZLE
WHAT'S WRONG, AMAJIKI?
YOU SHOULD BE CAPABLE OF MUCH MORE WITH YOUR QUIRK.
ARE YOU NERVOUS AGAIN...?
SLAM
GAHH !!
FINE. YOU TRIED. BACK IN LINE.

YOU'RE JUST KINDA CLUMSY WHEN IT COMES TO CONTROLLING YOUR QUIRK, TOGATA.

IT'S SUPER HARD, I'M TELLING YOU!! I WISH YOU ALL COULD GIVE IT A TRY!!

IT'S GOTTA BE AT LEAST FIVE TIMES TOUGHER THAN YOU THINK!!

HA HA HA HA

STOP MESSING AROUND, TOGATA!

YOUR FACE DIDN'T MAKE IT THROUGH!!

WHATEVER! I'M SURE I'LL PULL IT OFF NEXT TIME!!

CAW

YOU'RE... INCREDIBLE, MIRIO...

WHAT THE HECK?

YOU'RE GONNA BE A GREAT HERO SOMEDAY. BRIGHT AND SHINING, LIKE THE SUN.

YOU'RE GIVING ME WAY TOO MUCH CREDIT. IT'S NOT LIKE THAT AT ALL, MAN.

EVEN WHEN YOU SCREW UP...YOU STAY CHEERY... WITH EYES ON THE PRIZE. IT PUMPS EVERYONE UP TOO...

I JUST CAN'T... WHEN I EVEN *THINK* ABOUT FAILING...MY MIND GOES BLANK AND I FREEZE UP...

IT'S JUST, WHEN I SEE YOU OUT THERE, ALL NERVOUS...

...BUT YOU REFUSE TO BACK DOWN ANYWAY, I FEEL LIKE I DON'T WANNA LOSE TO YOU.

I'M NOT REALLY ALL THAT STRONG.

THE REASON I WORK SO HARD IS BECAUSE I'VE GOT YOU BY MY SIDE, TAMAKI.

BUT I KNOW THE TRUTH...

SAYING SILLY STUFF, LIKE HOW I'M THE SUN.

YOU'RE ALWAYS BUILDING ME UP WHILE UNDER-ESTIMATING YOURSELF.

LOSE...?

!

...YOU'RE A FUN GUY WITH A BRIGHT SIDE OF YOUR OWN.

THE TRUTH IS...

DEEP DOWN, YOU'VE GOT REAL TALENT.

YOU'RE GONNA BE EVEN GREATER THAN ANY REGULAR OL' SUN.

LET ME BORROW THAT WORD YOU USED...

ANYWAY... YOU GET THE PICTURE. BE CONFIDENT, TAMAKI!! YOU'RE...

GIVE IT UP. BECAUSE I'M...

YOU'LL OUTSHINE ANY SUN OUT THERE!!

...SUNEATER!

MY HERO ACADEMIA

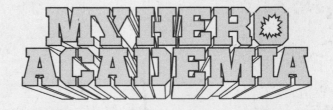

I CAN MANIFEST THE CHARACTERISTICS OF FOOD I EAT.
I'LL MAKE USE OF EVERYTHING ...
...MY QUIRK IS CAPABLE OF DOING!
CHUNKS OF MUSCLE AND THESE OCTOPUS TENTACLES CAN ABSORB ANY BLOW.
GUGUH
AND I CAN DEFEND AGAINST DAMAGE FROM HIS CRYSTALS BY LAYERING TOUGH SHELLS...
TCH...
YOU USE YOUR QUIRK WELL, BUT...
...IT'LL ONLY GET YOU SO FAR!!
EVERYTHING...
No. 141 – HASSAIKAI: BEHIND THE SCENES

FOR TWO AND A HALF YEARS NOW...
...I'VE BEEN PUSHING MY QUIRK'S LIMITS AT U.A.
I CAN CHANGE THE PARTS' SIZES.
MANI-FEST MULTIPLE PARTS AT ONCE.
CHOOSE WHICH TO USE AT ANY GIVEN POINT.
AND NOW I'M BRINGING EVERYTHING TO THE TABLE.
VAST HYBRID ...
CHIMERA

KRAKEN
!!

WHAM
WHAM
WHAM
WHAM
WHOA WHOA WHOA!!
I CAN DEAL WITH THEM MYSELF!
SO THAT'S WHAT HE MEANT!!
TIME TO EAT!!
TABE, WAKE UP!!
TWITCH

CHOMP
!!!
OCTOPUS ...
YUMMY.
WORMP

YUM.

YUM.

AND HIS STOMACH DIGESTS IT ALL BEFORE YOU KNOW IT!! THERE'S NO FILLING THAT GUY UP!!

HA HA HA!! HIS TEETH AND JAWS CAN TEAR THROUGH ANYTHING IN A FLASH!

BUT...IT'S FINE. I'LL JUST GIVE IT MY ALL!

ERASER KNEW WHAT A BAD MATCHUP IT'D BE FOR ME, SO HE TOOK THAT GUY OUT FIRST.

YOU HURTING YET?! I GOTTA SAY...

...YOU TWO ARE A MATCH MADE IN HEAVEN.

PLUS, I'M MOVING BETTER THAN THIS GUY EVER COULD!!
RIP
!!
THREE-ON-ONE, HUH? HA HA HA!!
JUST WHAT YOU WANTED, SUN-EATER!!
YOU THOUGHT YOU COULD PIN US DOWN BY WHIPPING THOSE BIG OL' TENTACLES AROUND?!
FWISH

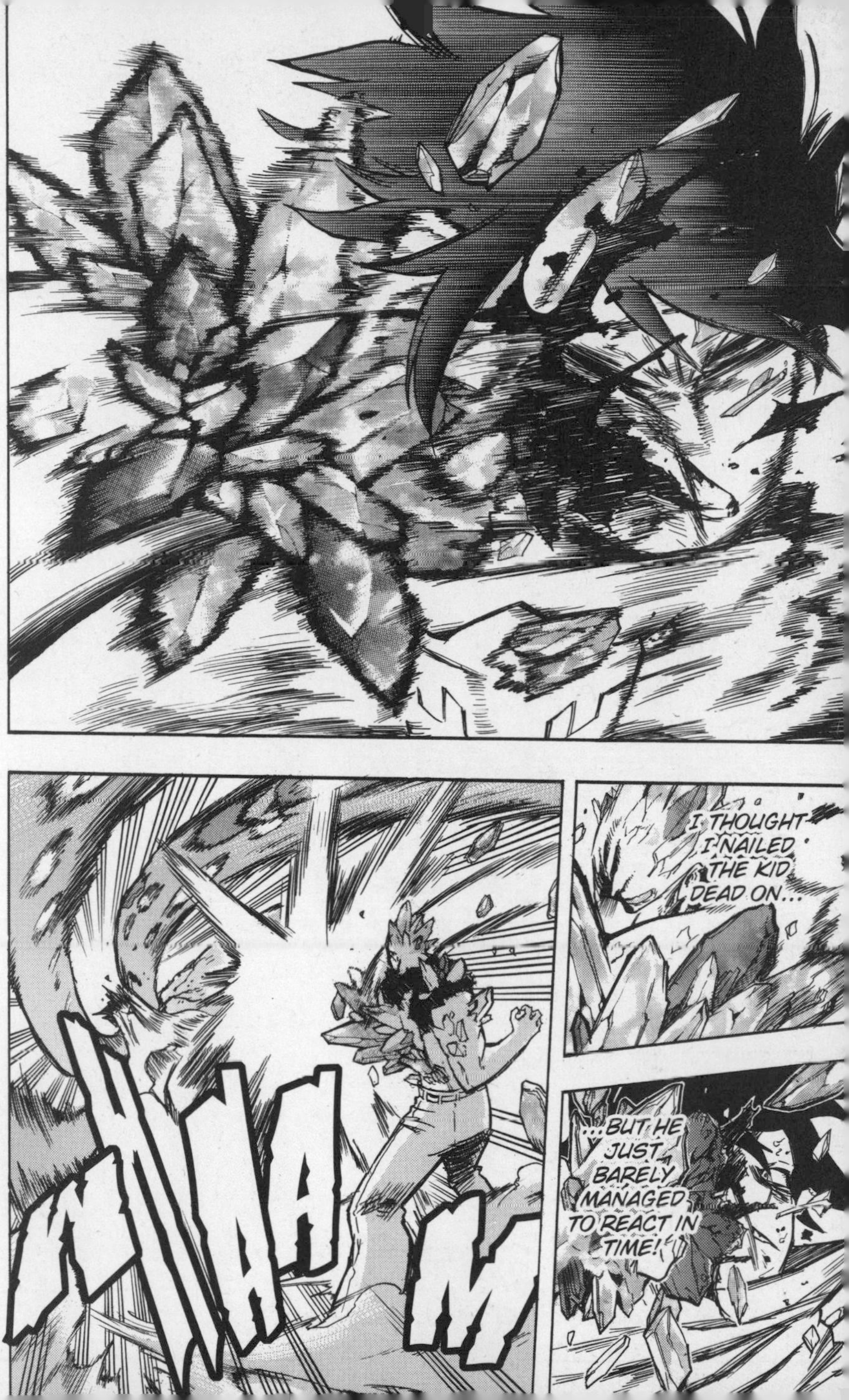
I THOUGHT I NAILED THE KID DEAD ON...
...BUT HE JUST BARELY MANAGED TO REACT IN TIME!
WHAM

...CAN'T BLOCK MY CRYSTALS, THOUGH.

A WEAK DEFENSE LIKE THAT...

...EATING ME DOWN TO NOTHING!!

HE'S...

YUMMY.

YUMMY.

CHOMP

CHOMP

IT'S IN THE TENTACLES NOW!! CHEW ON THAT!

THE COMMON OCTOPUS HAS A NEURO-TOXIN IN ITS SALIVA!

SQU

ELCH

...YOU'LL BE PARALYZED!

ONCE YOU DO...

SQUIRM

SQUIRM

SQUIRM

GUH

SNAP
SH
!!
I CAN'T STEAL THINGS WHEN THEY'RE TOO BIG.
BUT THESE LEFTOVERS ARE A DIFFERENT STORY.
POP
AM
THEIR TEAMWORK IS PERFECT!
GAHH!
WE MIGHT BE TRASH...
...BUT TRASH CAN FORM SOLID BONDS.
YOU'LL ALL BE ARRESTED.
WHETHER YOU BEAT ME OR NOT, YOU'VE GOT NO FUTURE.

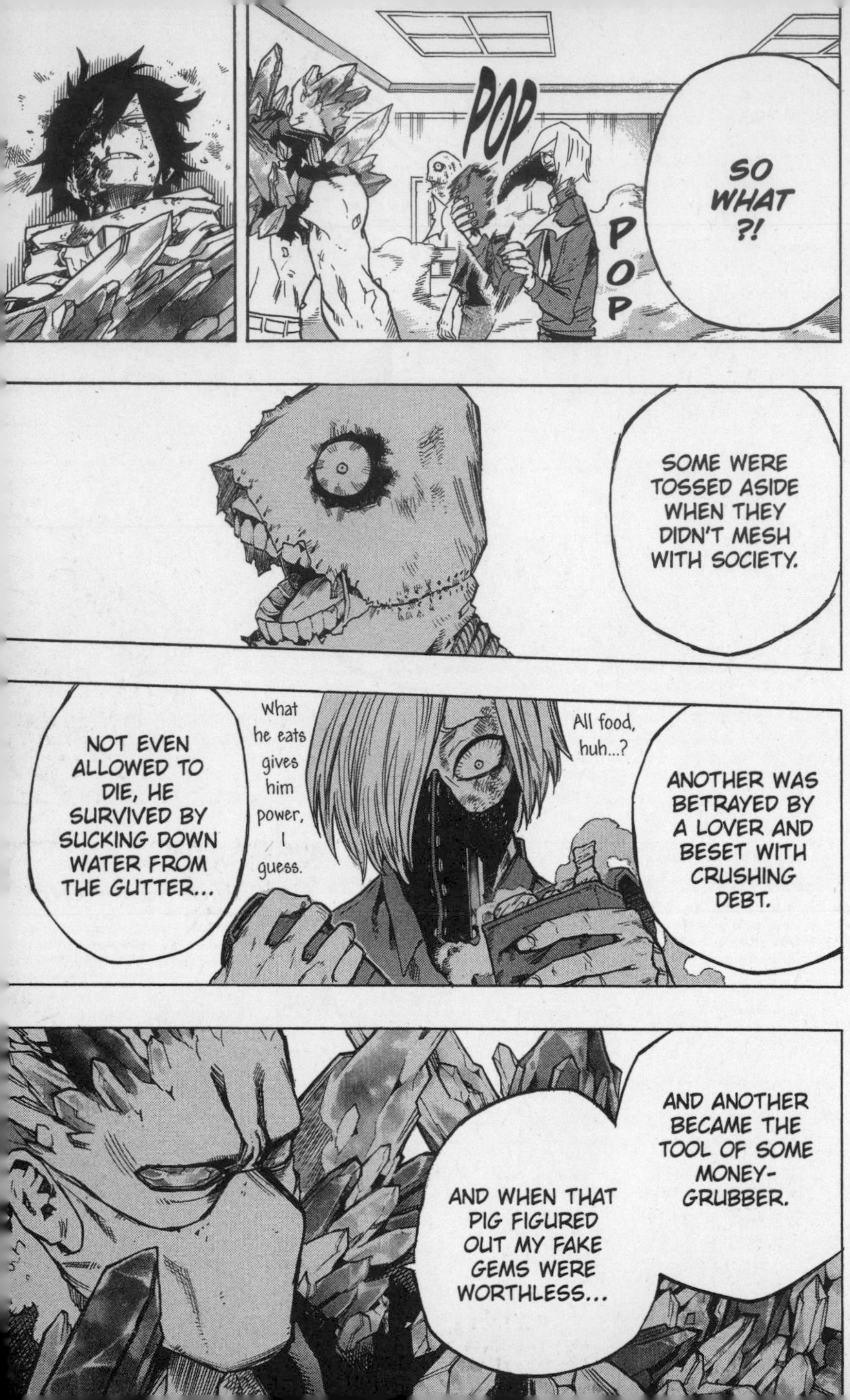

SO WHAT ?!

SOME WERE TOSSED ASIDE WHEN THEY DIDN'T MESH WITH SOCIETY.

NOT EVEN ALLOWED TO DIE, HE SURVIVED BY SUCKING DOWN WATER FROM THE GUTTER...

What he eats gives him power, I guess.

All food, huh...?

ANOTHER WAS BETRAYED BY A LOVER AND BESET WITH CRUSHING DEBT.

AND ANOTHER BECAME THE TOOL OF SOME MONEY-GRUBBER.

AND WHEN THAT PIG FIGURED OUT MY FAKE GEMS WERE WORTHLESS...

THAT'S WHEN HE CAME TO US...

COME JOIN THE HASSAIKAI.

YOU SHOULDN'T BE ROTTING AWAY ON THE STREETS.

AND BEATEN TO HELL AND BACK.

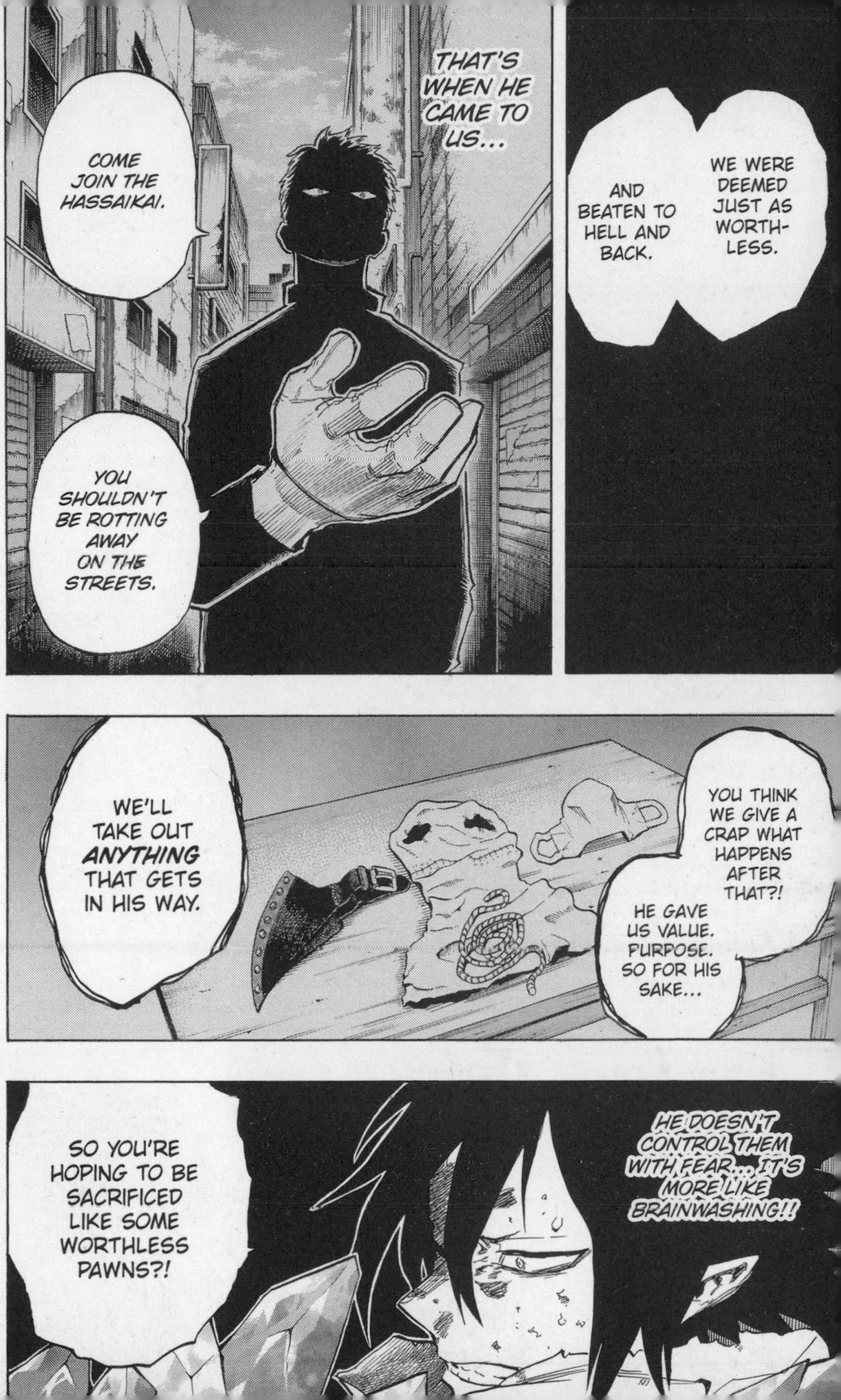

WE WERE DEEMED JUST AS WORTHLESS.

WE'LL TAKE OUT *ANYTHING* THAT GETS IN HIS WAY.

YOU THINK WE GIVE A CRAP WHAT HAPPENS AFTER THAT?!

HE GAVE US VALUE. PURPOSE. SO FOR HIS SAKE...

SO YOU'RE HOPING TO BE SACRIFICED LIKE SOME WORTHLESS PAWNS?!

HE DOESN'T CONTROL THEM WITH FEAR... IT'S MORE LIKE BRAINWASHING!!

A HERO COULD NEVER UNDER-STAND!
SHINK
PREPARE TO DIE!! YOU WON'T BE SO LUCKY THIS TIME!
WE MIGHT BE TRASH...
...BUT TRASH CAN FORM SOLID BONDS.
WITH YOUR BACK AGAINST THE WALL, YOU AIN'T GETTING AWAY FROM THIS ONE!!
MY ATTACKS GET GOBBLED UP.
AND MY DEFENSE GETS STRIPPED AWAY!!
SHF
SHF SHF SHF
IN THAT CASE...
FLIK

!!
WHAP
WHAP
WHAP
I'VE JUST GOTTA TEAR THEIR TEAMWORK...
...APART!
HIS LARCENY ONLY WORKS ON OBJECTS HE CAN SEE.
THAT'S WHY THE POLICE WOULDN'T DRAW THEIR GUNS ON HIM!
OWW!
BUT NOW THAT HIS EYES ARE OFF ME...!!
KR
AS
THOSE'RE MY...!!
THE PERFECT COUNTER!!
YOU...YOU ATE MY CRYSTALS!!
KRAK

THAT'S RIGHT!!
!!
YOU REALLY TRUST EACH OTHER, AND THAT WAS SOME KILLER TEAMWORK!!
EAT!! EAT!! EAT!! EAT!!

GUH
I MIGHT NOT UNDERSTAND YOUR GRIEF. YOUR RAGE. EVERYTHING THAT LED YOU HERE...
GUH GUH
FWO
OSH
BUT I KNOW ALL ABOUT SOLID BONDS!!

THH
BECAUSE FRIENDS DON'T EAT FRIENDS.
CHF
AND MY FRIENDS DON'T USE EACH OTHER!
CHF

THE FACES

TOYA SETSUNO ⟫
Cool dude. With the times.

⟪ YU HOJO
He shaves his head to make it easier to pump out those cystals.

SORAMITSU TABE ⟫
Always hungry.

BUT YOU WON'T BE ABLE TO MOVE ANYTIME SOON.

THOUGH YOU'VE BEEN POISONED, YOU WON'T DIE.

I'M TAKING THEM FOR NOW... THERE'S NO TELLING WHAT ELSE YOU MIGHT'VE HIDDEN UNDER THEM.

AS FOR THESE MASKS...

PHEW...

BADUM BADUM

TH UD

WHY'S THE FLOOR SO CLOSE TO MY FACE...?

HUH...

WORMP

I'VE GOTTA GET GOING.

EVERY-ONE'S PROBABLY FAR AHEAD BY NOW.

THAT TOOK LONGER THAN EXPECTED...!

No. 142 - Shield and Shield, Spear and Shield

MY HERO ACADEMIA

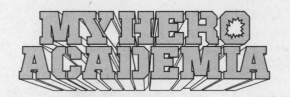

I HOPE TAMAKI IS OKAY... I CAN'T HELP BUT WORRY.

YEAH...

WHEN A GUY SAYS HE'S GOT YOUR BACK, A REAL MAN HAS JUST GOTTA BELIEVE!!

TAMAKI SWORE HE'D BE FINE, BUT THE KID'S WIMPY ACTIONS SOMETIMES SPEAK LOUDER THAN HIS WORDS.

EVEN THE UNDER-CLASSMEN HAVE NO FAITH IN HIM...

STILL, THOUGH!!

YOU SURE DO GO WITH THE FLOW, HUH?!

YEAH, HE'S GONNA BE FINE!!

YEAH, THE STAIRS!

A WAY BACK UP.

GIVE IT A REST, LOUD-MOUTH...

CAN'T WASTE EVEN A SECOND OF THE TIME SUNEATER BOUGHT US!

I'M WORRIED, BUT I GOTTA BELIEVE IN HIM!!

HIYAHHHH

...MUST MEAN THAT HE DOESN'T HAVE COMPLETE AWARENESS OR CONTROL OF THE BASEMENT.

THAT HE'S ALLOWED US TO COME THIS FAR WITHOUT INTERFERING...

ISN'T IT STRANGE THAT WE'VE SEEN NOTHING FROM THE GUY SHIFTING THE BASEMENT AROUND?

YOU'RE RIGHT... THE HALLS AREN'T ALL TWISTY ANYMORE!

ODD...

....!

IS THERE A LIMIT TO HOW MUCH HE CAN MONITOR AT ONCE?

...IS FOCUSING HIS ATTENTION ON THEM?

PERHAPS OUR VILLAIN...

SUNEATER'S BACK THERE, AND THE OFFICERS ARE UP ABOVE...

HE HASN'T BECOME THE FACILITY ITSELF. RATHER, HE'S SNEAKING THROUGH THE WALLS, WATCHING AND LISTENING.

THIS IS JUST A THEORY, BUT I THINK HE LITERALLY DOVE INTO THE BASEMENT TO CONTROL IT.

HE MUST STICK HIS REAL EYES OR EARS OUT TO OBSERVE...

SO WHEN HE SHIFTS THINGS AROUND TO SLOW US DOWN, THERE'S A CHANCE HIS REAL BODY IS NEARBY.

GLARE

EVEN IF THEY'RE SCUM, THOSE THREE WERE SUPPOSED TO BE REAL STRONG!

KRIK KRIK

THEY ONLY MANAGED TO SLOW DOWN ONE GUY...?!

RIGHT... IT'S BECAUSE OF HIM!!
FWOOOOOO
YOU SHOULD'VE JUST COME QUIETLY...
...INSTEAD OF RUSHING ALL AT ONCE TO STOP US.
KIND OF A CRAZY MOVE.
OH, WE AIN'T CRAZY.
EVERY-ONE YOU'RE ARRESTING IS PERFECTLY SANE.
IF WE CAME QUIETLY, OVERHAUL WOULD END US.
OVER-? YOU MEAN CHISAKI?
YEP.
OVERHAUL'S BEEN HIS MONIKER EVER SINCE THE OLD BOSS GOT SICK AND HE STARTED TAKING OVER THE OPERATION.

HE HATED WHEN THEY BRANDED US A "DESIGNATED VILLAIN ORGANIZATION."

HE DIDN'T WANT US TO BE VILLAINS AND THOUGHT HASSAIKAI SHOULD FOLLOW THE ESTABLISHED TRADITIONS.

HE WAS ALWAYS SEARCHING FOR A WAY OUR KIND COULD SURVIVE IN THIS AGE.

THE BOSS HAD A LOT OF RESPECT FOR THE TRADITIONAL METHODS OF RUNNING A GANG.

DECIDING ALL ON HIS OWN TO TAKE THE GANG IN A DIRECTION THAT DOESN'T SUIT US... RUNNING WILD LIKE THAT? THAT'S ALL HIM.

AS FOR OVERHAUL... USING VILLAIN NAMES... BRINGING REAL VILLAINS INTO THE OPERATION...

HE'S THE BOSS WE RESPECTED.

SO YOU'RE NOT EXACTLY FANS OF CHISAKI...

...BUT YOU DON'T BELIEVE HE'LL BE CAUGHT.

HEY...

AND I'M DAMN SURE THAT THE ONE WHO MESSED UP THE OLD BOSS SO BAD HE CAN'T TALK NO MORE WAS...

AND GUYS LIKE THAT...? THEY'RE STRONG.

Y'SEE, WHACKJOBS LIKE HIM DON'T TROUBLE THEMSELVES WITH CONSE-QUENCES.

RIGHT...!

HE'S AIMING FOR ME!
OF COURSE...
HE DOESN'T WANT TO BE "SEEN"...
SWI
RL
ERASER !!
HEH HEH... IF THOSE THREE COULDN'T CUT IT...
I'VE JUST GOTTA REDUCE THEIR NUMBERS...
...ONE AT A TIME!!

FAT!!
IF THIS JERK GETS HIS WAY...
...THE TIME TAMAKI BOUGHT US'LL BE ALL FOR NOTHING, ERASER.
YOU'VE GOTTA ERASE HIM!
THANKS!
DON'T MENTION IT!!

ROLL
ROLL
ROLL
NNN ...!!
GAHH !!
WHAT THE HECK?! IS THAT A BABY CHICK?!
I DOVE IN TOO, HOPING TO PROTECT SENSEI...
...CUZ I KNEW I WOULDN'T TAKE ANY DAMAGE!!
BUT THEN I SANK INTO YOU, FAT...
IT IS WHAT IT IS!! BUT STAY ON GUARD, NOW...
TOMP

A FIST!!
IT AIN'T BREAKING ME!!
KASH
UNBREAKABLE!!

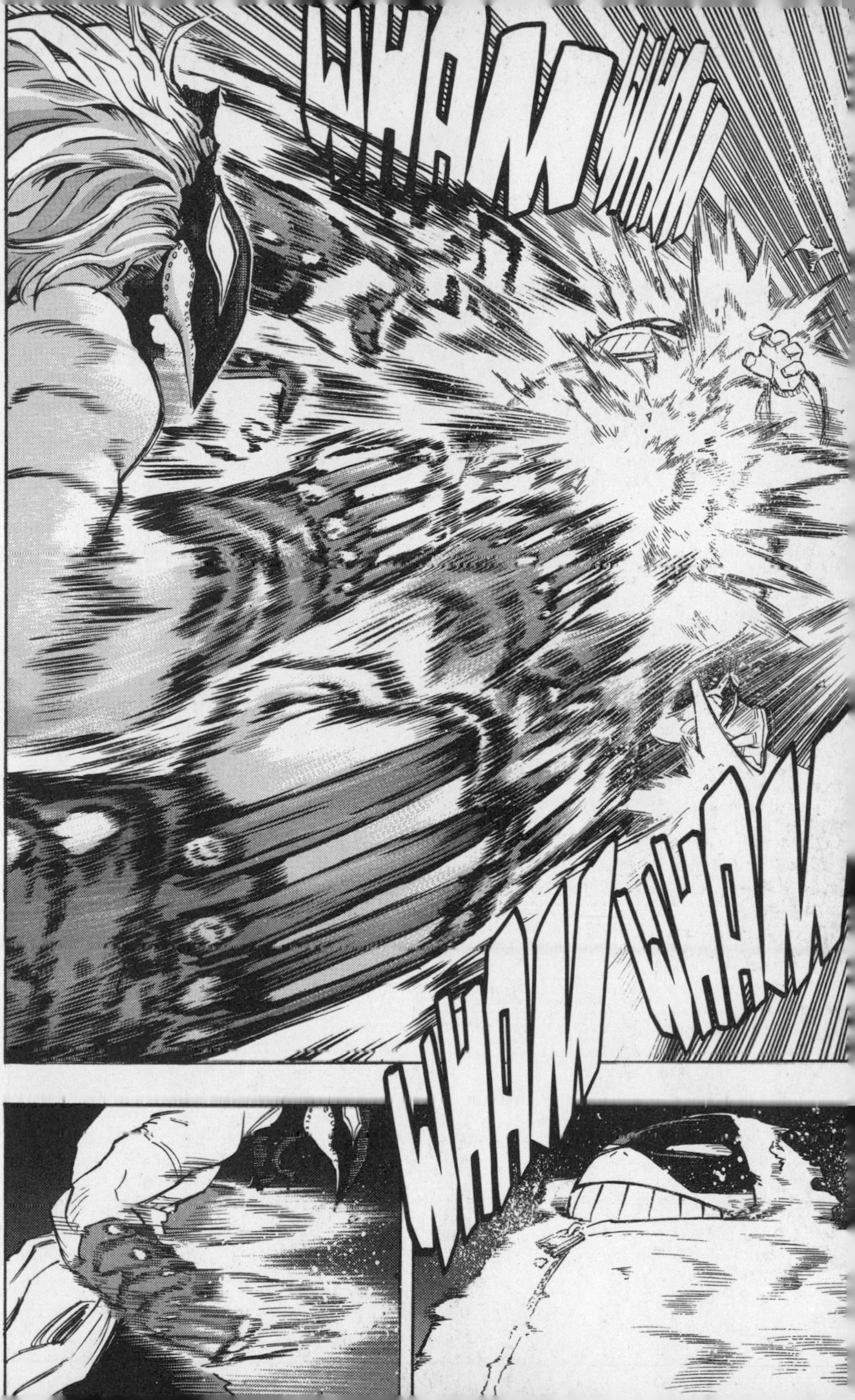
WHAM WHAM
WHAM WHAM WHAM

WHOEVER'S GOT THE WEAPON WINS, RIGHT? THAT AIN'T A REAL FIGHT.

...THERE'S SOMETHING REALLY TASTELESS ABOUT BRINGING A GUN OR A KNIFE TO A FIGHT.

I THINK...

FSHHH

RED...

FSSHHH

MEN'RE MEANT TO RIP EACH OTHER APART WITH THEIR OWN POWER. YOU FEEL ME?

KRIK
HAHH!
HAHH!

HUH?! A BARRIER?!
WHAT'S GOING ON?!
FWIP
FAT GUM AND A BOY WHO CAN HARDEN HIS BODY...
JUST TWO... HMPH!
AND BOTH WITH DEFENSE-ORIENTED QUIRKS.
NOTHING BUT PUNKS. WHAT A SHAME, RAPPA.

GUH!
BAM
BAM
BAM
BAM
KOFF...
EVEN MY FAT'S FEELING THOSE IMPACTS... EACH ONE'S LIKE A BULLET!!
DEFENSE ORIENTED, HUH? GUY'S BARELY STANDING AFTER THAT.
STILL, IT'S IMPRESSIVE THAT HE'S STILL IN ONE PIECE, RIGHT?
I NEVER SAW REGISTERED QUIRKS FOR THESE TWO... THEY MUST BE OUTSIDERS.
A BARRAGE OF BULLET PUNCHES PLUS BARRIERS... THAT'S ONE NASTY COMBO THEY GOT GOING...

WE ARE A SPEAR AND SHIELD...
...UP AGAINST TWO SHIELDS.
WAIT... SO THIS AIN'T GONNA BE A REAL FIGHT? THAT SUCKS...
ESPECIALLY SINCE CALLING THE BOY A SHIELD...
...GIVES HIM TOO MUCH CREDIT...
HAHH...
HAHH...
GRRRRAH!
I'M CRACKED...!!
IT HURTS!! I COULDN'T TAKE THOSE HITS!

DAMMIT...!! I THOUGHT I'D GOTTEN STRONGER!!

ONE MORE FLURRY LIKE THAT, THOUGH, AND I'M TOAST...

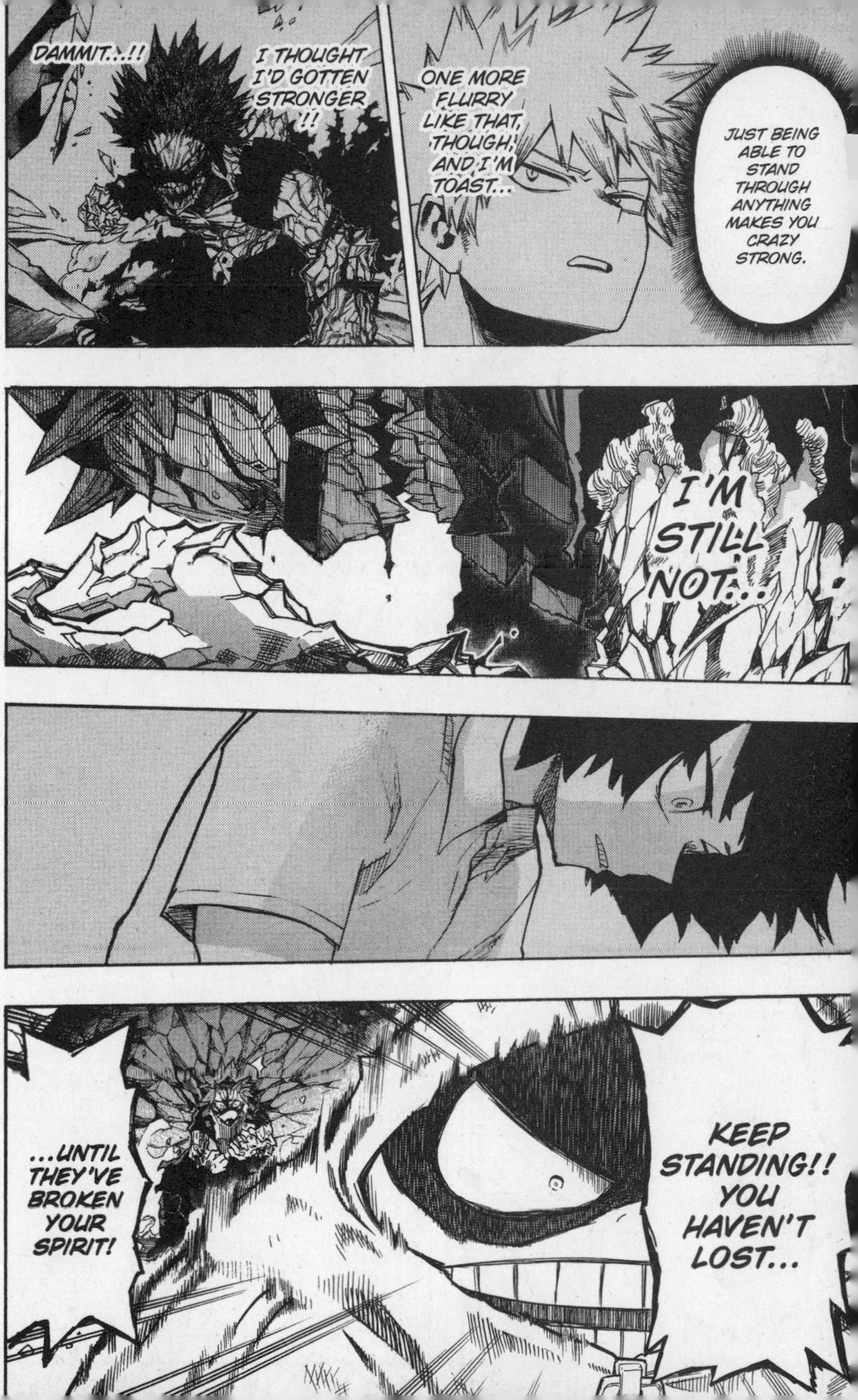

JUST BEING ABLE TO STAND THROUGH ANYTHING MAKES YOU CRAZY STRONG.

I'M STILL NOT...

...UNTIL THEY'VE BROKEN YOUR SPIRIT!

KEEP STANDING!! YOU HAVEN'T LOST...

THIS FATSO REALLY GETS IT. GOOD FOR HIM!

THEY BELIEVE THEY CAN WIN. YOU MUST BE PLEASED, RAPPA.

TAKING DOWN VILLAINS IS ALL ABOUT HOW FAST YOU CAN MAKE 'EM LOSE THE WILL TO FIGHT! IF YOU THROW IN THE TOWEL FIRST, WHAT THEN?

LET'S BEAT THESE PAWNS DOWN...

AND REJOIN THE GROUP!!

KENDO RAPPA 》》

He joined the world of street fighting as an act of rebellion against his overly strict parents.

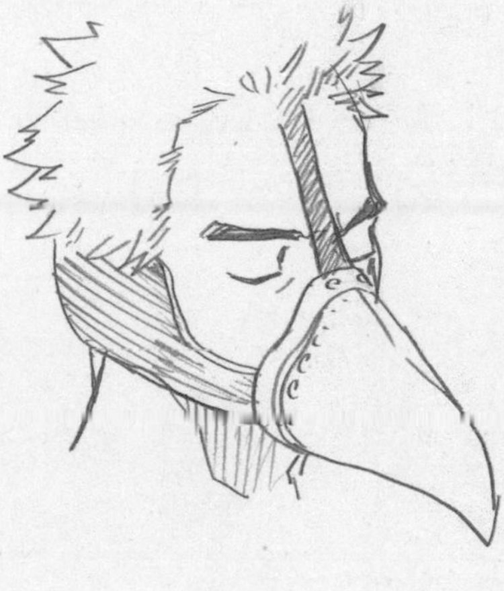

《《 HEKIJI TENGAI

Rappa's tendency to challenge people to fights was getting obnoxious, so Chisaki brought Tengai into the Hassai gang to serve as Rappa's babysitter of sorts. He's the newest member of the gang. Used to be a devout Buddhist.

No. 143 - Let's Rumble, Rappa!!
OOH, THIS IS ABOUT TO GET FUN!
TENGAI, TAKE THIS CRAP DOWN AND CUT IT OUT.
IT'S NOT LIKE I NEEDED A BARRIER IN THE FIRST PLACE.
CLAK
CLAK
DO NOT SUBMIT TO SELFISH DESIRES.
AND DO NOT FORGET MASTER OVERHAUL'S ORDERS.
WE MAKE THE PERFECT TEAM.
OUR COMBINED STRENGTH IS MORE THAN CAPABLE OF BRINGING THEM DOWN.

ZOOM

WHAM

WHAM WHAM WHAM WHAM WHAM

AS LONG AS I GET TO FIGHT IN DEATH MATCHES, I COULDN'T CARE LESS.

OVERJERK'S THE ONE WHO DECIDED WE SHOULD BE A TEAM.

ENOUGH OF THAT, YOU BATTLE-CRAZED LUNATIC...

WE GOT AN UNDERSTANDING, THEN? YOU'RE ALL RIGHT, FOR A SHUT-IN.

Great!

AS YOU WISH. HOWEVER, YOU BETTER FINISH THE JOB.

AND IT'S NOT OVERJERK. IT'S MASTER OVERHAUL.

!!

POW POW

GUH!!

POW POW POW

AT THIS RATE, HE'LL BREAK ME LITTLE BY LITTLE TILL I'M DONE!

PLUS, THE SHOCK OF EACH BLOW IS DAMAGING ME, DESPITE MY QUIRK!!

AND DODGING HIS BARRAGE OF BLOWS IS IMPOSSIBLE.

KOFF!

KEEPING TRACK BY SIGHT'S NOT GONNA WORK... HE'S TOO FAST.

SKF'S KF

MY POWER JUST AIN'T ENOUGH TO DEAL WITH SOMETHING THAT TOUGH!

IT FELT LIKE A STEEL WALL WHEN I HIT IT...

...THERE'S NO DOUBT THAT OTHER GUY'LL SHIELD HIS PAL IF THINGS GET HAIRY.

AND DESPITE THEIR LITTLE FALLING-OUT A SECOND AGO...

...WE AIN'T WINNING THIS! UNLESS WE TAKE THAT GUY OUT...

LITTLE KIRISHIMA'S ALREADY HURT REAL BAD...

NOT TO MENTION...

FAT...!!

SO WHO'S GONNA CRY UNCLE FIRST? YOU AND YOUR ARMS, OR ME AND MY BODY?

I USED TO BE A ROUGH-'N'-TUMBLE BRAWLER MYSELF, WAY BACK.

SCREW THIS UP, AND I'M DEAD...

FWIP

I HAVE NO CHOICE. I GOTTA DO IT...

WHICH'S STRONGER? SPEAR OR SHIELD?

SHUDDER

SHUDDER

IT'S RAPPA, RIGHT? IT'S BEEN A GOOD LONG WHILE SINCE I FELT ANYTHING AT ALL FROM AN ATTACK.

HA HA

IF I DON'T PULL THIS OFF...
...I'M DEFINITELY DEAD!!
LET'S RUMBLE!!
RAPPA!!
YOU'RE MY KINDA GUY, FATSO!
TENGAI!! NO BARRIERS!!
RIGHT.
GREAT! EVERY-ONE'S BEING REAL COOPERATIVE TODAY!!
FSSHH

FAT!
FAT !!
PROTECTING ME, LIKE THAT...
EVEN THOUGH THOSE PUNCHES'RE CLEARLY TOO MUCH FOR HIM!!
I WAS SUPPOSED TO HAVE GOTTEN STRONGER.
SO I JUMPED RIGHT IN.
BUT THAT ULTIMATE MOVE I WAS SO PROUD OF GOT SMASHED UP LIKE IT WAS NOTHING!
NOW I'M JUST IN THE WAY!!
WHAT'M I EVEN DOING?

SH
RIP RIP
CAN I EVEN MAKE IT THROUGH THIS?!
BAM
SHOOT! 'SREALLY HURTING NOW!! HE'S ALL FIRED UP!
BAN

DON'T LET ME DOWN, FATSO!
JUST STAND THERE FOR ME.
WHAM
I'M JUST GETTING WARMED UP!
BAM BAM
WHAT CAN I EVEN DO NOW?!
THERE'S GOTTA BE SOME-THING!!
SHF
FAT GUM'S GONNA DIE!!
AND IT'S ALL MY FAULT!
I'M JUST A PLAIN GUY WITH NOTHING TO OFFER!!
WHEN MY HARDENING CRACKS, I'VE GOT NOTHING!!

I'M USELESS ...!!

THERE'S NO COMING BACK FROM A PLACE LIKE THAT.

HOW PITIFUL...!

HIS EYES ARE STAINED WITH FEAR.

THAT BOY... HE'S ALREADY A LOST CAUSE.

JUST A BIT MORE...

AND CANCELIN' OUT THE HITS TAKES A MOUNTAIN OF ENERGY, Y'SEE. IT BURNS OFF ALL THAT FAT SERVIN' AS MY SHIELD!

CUZ EVERY ONE OF THEM BLOWS WAS GETTIN' ABSORBED, SINKIN' INTO ME!!

EVERY BLOW GETS STORED...

SO MY DEFENSE IS GETTIN' EATEN AWAY, BUT...

AW, C'MON!! HANG IN THERE, BUDDY!!

...IT'LL BE THE DEATH OF YA...

IF YER THINKIN' I'M JUST A SHIELD...

....!

...THAT'LL CRACK ANY SHIELD OUT THERE!

I'M FORGIN' A SPEAR...

BUT HE'S WORN MY SHIELD DOWN TO NOTHING... GOTTA UNLEASH ALL THAT STORED POWER, BUT...I DON'T KNOW IF I CAN MAKE IT...!!

THAT WAS THE PLAN, ANYWAY...

RAPPA! HE'S UP TO SOMETHING!

FINISH HIM, NOW!!

I GOTTA KNOW!!

IF YOU'RE STILL ALIVE, SHOW ME WHATEVER IT IS YOU'VE GOT!!

RIP

WHAT ?!
RED ...
WHAM
WHAM WHAM
?!
HE'S TAKING IT?!
AFTER GETTING BLOWN AWAY SO EASILY BEFORE?
WHAM WHAM

HARDENING RIGHT BACK UP AFTER BREAKING!!
KRAK
SKF SKF
WAY TO GO, KID!!
AH-HH-HH-HH!

VWOOM
WHAM
WORMP
WHAT WASTED EFFORT, THOUGH...
NO TECHNIQUE CAN OVER-COME MY DEFENSE.
A BAR-RIER?!
I DEPLOYED ONE, NATURALLY.
!
HE CAN ONLY SUBMIT.
AIN'T NO WASTED EFFORT!

SO NOW IT'S YOU PROTECTIN' ME, LITTLE GUY...?
FEELS KINDA INSULTIN', HONESTLY...
BUT NOW THIS BIG OLD SPEAR IS READY FOR ACTION!!

Just an ordinary hoodie and mask. All my costume's gotta do is stretch a lot.
Nothing else matters, yeah?
I mean...right...?

NO.144 - RED RIOT, PART 1
BWOOM
TAKE THIS STINKIN' BARRIER DOWN, TENGAI!!
SO THAT'S THE REASON FOR THE ATTACK.
IT WASN'T WASTED EFFORT?
THAT'S NOT IT...

I WAS JUST SCARED...

AGAIN...

HEY, I HEARD ABOUT YOU.

*SIGN: MUSTAFU MIDDLE SCHOOL

BUT...I CAN'T, REALLY.

THEN WE JUST GOTTA SPEND IT ALL BEFORE THAT HAPPENS. NO ONE'LL CATCH US!

TMP

CREATING MONEY WOULD BE WRONG...!

BESIDES, THE TRANSFORMATION WEARS OFF PRETTY QUICKLY.

YOU'VE GOT A QUIRK THAT CAN TRANSFORM LEAVES INTO OTHER THINGS, RIGHT?

THAT'S PERFECT!

WHY DON'TCHA GO AND MAKE SOME 10,000-YEN BILLS FOR US? MY WALLET'S FEELING A LITTLE LIGHT THIS MONTH.

HEY, HEY!! THREATENING YOUR UNDER-CLASSMAN FOR POCKET CHANGE?
THAT AIN'T MANLY AT ALL!
WHOZZAT?
THAT THIRD-YEAR, KIRISHIMA.
HERE HE COMES.
SHINK
DON'T WORRY.
TMP TMP
TMP TMP
WHAM
FWIP
YOWWWWWW!!
HE'S NOT MUCH, REALLY.
HIS QUIRK JUST MAKES HIM SLIGHTLY HARDER.
JERKS!
AS WE WERE SAYING...
GAH! WAIT RIGHT THERE!

YOU MEAN WATCHING YOU STICK YOUR NOSE WHERE IT DOESN'T BELONG AGAIN? YEAH.

YOU GET A LOAD OF THAT?!

MY FRIENDS!

RUSTL

CUT IT OUT, EI.

AS LONG AS A MAN'S GOT A CHIVALROUS HEART, HIS QUIRK'S GOT NOTHING TO DO WITH IT!!

THAT'S SOME REALLY OLD-FASHIONED THINKING.

AND IT'S LIKE THE PROS SAY!! YOUR BODY STARTS MOVING BEFORE YOU'VE GOT TIME TO THINK!! MEANING...

ZOOSH

THAT'S WHAT CHIVALROUS HERO CRIMSON RIOT ALWAYS SAID!!

WHAT'S SHE SAYING TO 'EM...?

THAT'S MINA ASHIDO, FROM CLASS 3-4...

WHAT THE HECK?

THEY'RE LEAVING!

NOW THEY'RE BREAK-DANCING TOGETHER.

SO THEY'RE ALL FRIENDS NOW?

SHE'S GOING PLACES. THAT'S FOR SURE.

HM?!

FWUMP

SURE THING!

MINA, WANNA GO TO THAT STORE TODAY?

There y'are!

What was that about?

AND HER QUIRK IS STRONG AND FLASHY, TO BOOT.

SHE'S GOT KILLER PHYSICAL REFLEXES!! PLUS, SHE'S GREAT WITH PEOPLE.

I HEAR ASHIDO IS APPLYING TO U.A.

MEANWHILE, MY QUIRK IS JUST HARDENING. KINDA BORING, TO BE HONEST.

ASHIDO IS TOTALLY SUITED TO BE A HERO IN THIS DAY AND AGE.

IT'S ALL ABOUT THE ENTERTAINMENT FACTOR AND APPROVAL RATINGS.

NOWADAYS PEOPLE EXPECT DIFFERENT THINGS FROM HEROES THAN THEY USED TO.

私立結田府中学校

"AS LONG AS A MAN'S GOT A CHIVALROUS HEART, HIS QUIRK'S GOT NOTHING TO DO WITH IT!!"
WHICH'S WHY I'M TRAINING WITH ALL MY MIGHT TO MAKE UP FOR MY QUIRK!!
THAT'S WHAT I TELL MYSELF, ANYWAY...
SPEAKING OF HIGH SCHOOLS, SHOULD WE GO FOR IT TOO? THE ILLUSTRIOUS U.A.!!
DUMMY. WE'RE WAY TOO PLAIN TO BE HEROES. GOTTA RULE THAT OUT FROM THE START, Y'KNOW.
HOW ABOUT YOU, EI? GONNA COME TO DROID TECHNICAL HIGH WITH US?
OH... WELL, KINDA HAVEN'T DECIDED YET. HA HA...
TOP HIGH SCHOOL CHOICES SURVEY
U.A. HIGH

I'M SO LAME.
BUT SEEING ASHIDO GOT ME THINKING.
IF I HAD SOME STRONG, FLASHY QUIRK LIKE HERS...
...MAYBE I'D ALSO HAVE THE CONFIDENCE TO GO FOR U.A.'S HERO COURSE?
SHAKA
TOKYO'S LOOKING AT ANOTHER SUNNY DAY TOMORROW.
LOOKS LIKE WE'VE GOT A FEW MORE SCORCHERS IN STORE!!
WHAT'S... GOING ON?

THE SPRINGER HERO AGENCY...
WHERE IS IT?
WE HAVE A LETTER HERE.
RADIO NAME: ALM IGHT.
EEK!
I KNOW THEM FROM SCHOOL...!!!
中地 内科
SHF
YOU WON'T TELL ME?
THE OTHER DAY, ON MY COMMUTE ...
...I SAW ALL MIGHT.
KRIK

KRAKK
30
NO... SOMEONE...
NO HEROES ON PATROL! BUT NOW?! OF ALL TIMES?!
CRAP!
SHNK
YOU...
YOU DO IT!
CHCHF
WHY WON'T YOU TELL ME...?
JUST DO IT...

TURN AT THE CORNER!
THEN LEFT AT THE AVENUE!! THE AGENCY'S TWO KILOMETERS AWAY!
...
THANKS!
ALL FOR MY MASTER...
TOMP

YOU GAVE HIM RANDOM DIRECTIONS, SO LET'S GET OUTTA HERE NOW.

HE WOULDA KILLED US IF YOU HADN'T SHOWN UP.

WAHHHHH

THANK YOU, MINAAAA!

WAHHHHHHH

WAHHHH! TOO SCARY!

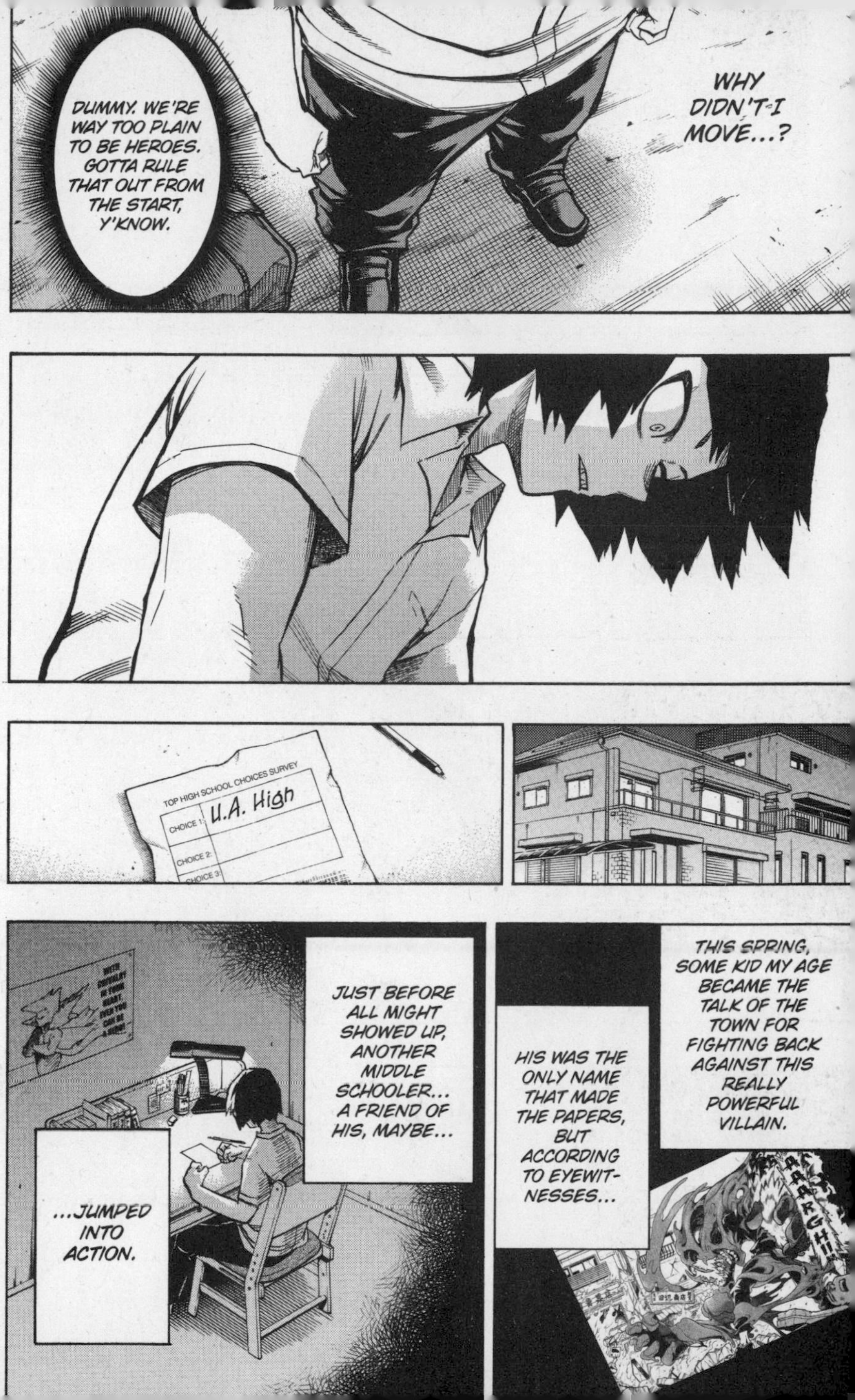

DUMMY. WE'RE WAY TOO PLAIN TO BE HEROES. GOTTA RULE THAT OUT FROM THE START, Y'KNOW.

WHY DIDN'T I MOVE...?

TOP HIGH SCHOOL CHOICES SURVEY

CHOICE 1 | U.A. High
CHOICE 2 |
CHOICE 3 |

...JUMPED INTO ACTION.

JUST BEFORE ALL MIGHT SHOWED UP, ANOTHER MIDDLE SCHOOLER... A FRIEND OF HIS, MAYBE...

HIS WAS THE ONLY NAME THAT MADE THE PAPERS, BUT ACCORDING TO EYEWITNESSES...

THIS SPRING, SOME KID MY AGE BECAME THE TALK OF THE TOWN FOR FIGHTING BACK AGAINST THIS REALLY POWERFUL VILLAIN.

I'M NOT MAKING UP FOR SQUAT WITH MY SPIRIT...
CUZ MY SPIRIT'S LACKING TOO...
I COULDN'T JUMP INTO ACTION EVEN WHEN PEOPLE WERE IN REAL DANGER.
SKRITCH SKRITCH
I'M...
TOP HIGH SCHOOL CHOICES SURVEY
CHOICE 1:
CHOICE 2:
CHOICE 3:
CLASS: 1 Eijiro Kirishima
I'M NOT A MAN. I'M NOTHING.

THE COSTUME

EIJIRO KIRISHIMA'S COSTUME

CHIVALROUS HEADGEAR!!

Made to protect the nose and chin during head-on assaults!! But it'll break apart relatively quickly!!

CHIVALROUS SHOULDER GUARDS!!

Emphasizes Kirishima's intensity! Easier to move around in than the previous versions!!

CHIVALROUS ARM COVERS!!

Kirishima worries about accidentally hurting people with his bare skin when holding or carrying them!! These new arm covers are made with polyurethane!!

CHIVALROUS CLOTH!!

Whatever he wears is bound to get destroyed anyway, so Kirishima opted for ragged cloth from the start!! Torn-up clothing like this is practically a badge of honor for manly men!!

I AIN'T EVEN A MAN.

HERO? YEAH, RIGHT.

NO.145 - RED RIOT; PART 2

BUT WHEN THINGS GOT HAIRY...

ALL I DID WAS TALK BIG.

I SHOWED MY TRUE COLORS.

WHEN IT WAS TIME TO PUT MY LIFE ON THE LINE...

...AND DECIDE TO TAKE THAT NEXT STEP FORWARD ANYWAY... THEY'RE THE ONES WHO CAN BE HEROES.

THOSE WHO STARE DOWN DEATH...

WITH CHIVALRY IN YOUR HEART, EVEN YOU CAN BE A HERO!

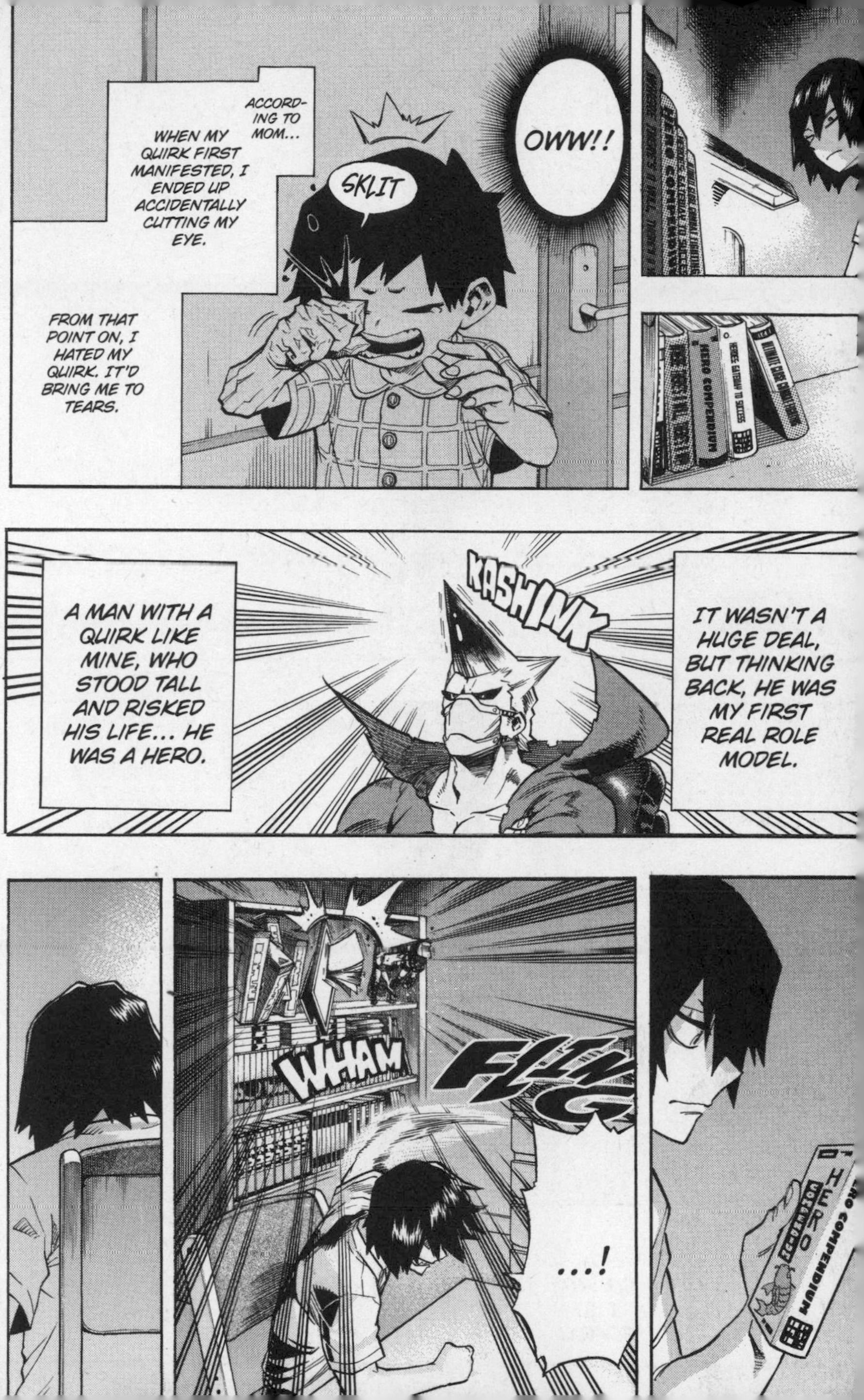

HERO COMPENDIUM
HEROES: GATEWAY TO SUCCESS
ACCORDING TO MOM...
OWW!!
SKLIT
WHEN MY QUIRK FIRST MANIFESTED, I ENDED UP ACCIDENTALLY CUTTING MY EYE.
FROM THAT POINT ON, I HATED MY QUIRK. IT'D BRING ME TO TEARS.
KASHINK
A MAN WITH A QUIRK LIKE MINE, WHO STOOD TALL AND RISKED HIS LIFE... HE WAS A HERO.
IT WASN'T A HUGE DEAL, BUT THINKING BACK, HE WAS MY FIRST REAL ROLE MODEL.
...!
HERO COMPENDIUM
FLING
WHAM

OH...

WHIRR

!!

JOLT

IT'S SOME EXTRA FOOTAGE THAT CAME WITH A BOOK OF GREAT HEROES...

I GOT THAT FOR MY BIRTHDAY A WHILE BACK.

HERO BIOS

50 GREAT HEROES

THAT AIN'T IT!!

YES!! I'M READY!!

P-PARDON ME! THE FIRST QUESTION, THEN...

GUESS I NEVER WATCHED THIS...?

JOLT

WHO DO YOU THINK I AM?!

OF COURSE I GET SCARED.

WITH CHIVALRY IN YOUR HEART, EVEN YOU CAN BE A HERO!

MR. CRIMSON. SOME WOULD SAY THAT YOU HAVE A STRONG REPUTATION FOR BEING A RECKLESS HERO, COMPARED TO OTHERS.

AREN'T YOU SCARED EVERY TIME YOU CHARGE HEADLONG INTO DANGER?

OH...

ONLY IDIOTS AND BEEEEP!!

AIN'T NO ONE OUT THERE WHO FACES DOWN DEATH WITHOUT FEAR.

THAT AIN'T IT!

YOU COULD HARDLY BE BLAMED FOR THAT. AND NOW, WITH ROCKETING CRIME RATES EVERYWHERE...

I REMEMBER.

THERE WERE SOME LIVES I COULDA SAVED BUT DIDN'T.

BACK IN MY SIDEKICK DAYS...

IT WAS MY WEAK SPIRIT THAT DOOMED THOSE FOLKS.

I HESITATED FOR A SECOND, SEE.

I DIDN'T UNDERSTAND AS A LITTLE KID. NOT REALLY.

I JUST SAW HIM AS THIS AWESOME DUDE, CHARGING FORWARD AT FULL SPEED...

BUT I KNOW SOMETHING SCARIER THAN DEATH...

VILLAINS'RE SCARED OF DYING TOO!

THE MESSAGE DIDN'T SINK IN.

WHAT IS CHIVALRY?

IN YOUR OWN WORDS...

WE ASSOCIATE IT WITH MEN, BUT IT AIN'T ABOUT GENDER!

A STRONG SPIRIT.

IT AIN'T ABOUT CONFIDENCE OR BEING FEARLESS.

NONE OF THAT!!

ONCE THAT DECISION'S MADE...

I'M A HERO, SO I PROTECT PEOPLE!

...I GOTTA PUT MY LIFE ON THE LINE FOR IT!!

THE PAIN I COULDN'T PREVENT.

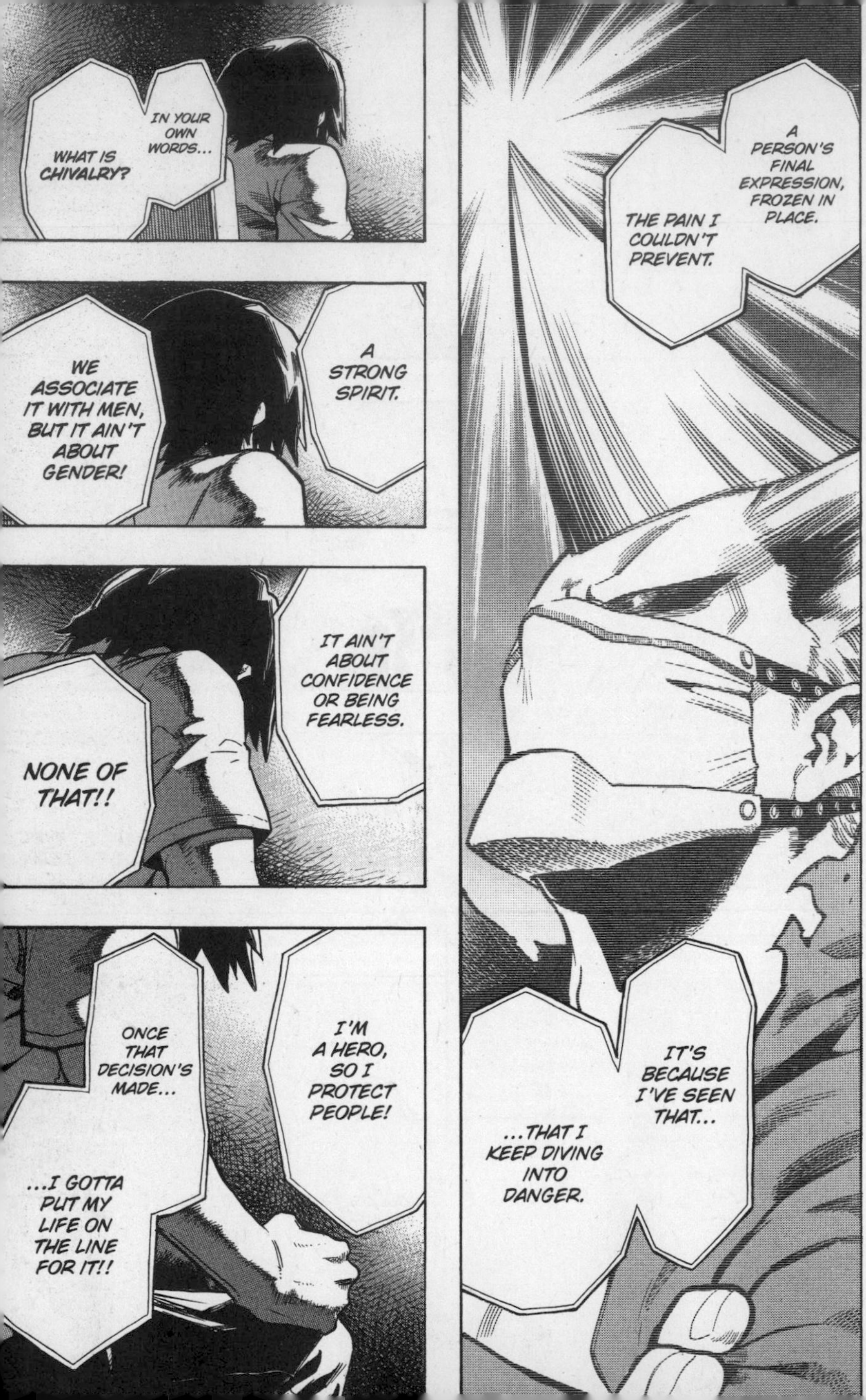

A PERSON'S FINAL EXPRESSION, FROZEN IN PLACE.

IT'S BECAUSE I'VE SEEN THAT...

...THAT I KEEP DIVING INTO DANGER.

IT'S ABOUT LIVING WITHOUT REGRET.
THAT'S WHAT CHIVALRY IS TO ME!
SERIOUSLY, EI?
TOP HIGH SCHOOL CHOICES SURVEY
CHOICE 1: U.A. High
CHOICE 2:
CHOICE 3:
CLASS: 1 Eijiro Kirishima

NO GOING BACK NOW.
NOT FOR ME.
SORRY!
I...SAW YOU TWO, WHEN IT ALL WENT DOWN.
BUT I GOT SCARED AND FROZE UP...!
WHO'S... HE?
FROM CLASS 3-1, I THINK...
DON'T WORRY ABOUT IT. ANYONE WOULD'VE BEEN SCARED.
MINA'S TOTALLY THE EXCEPTION TO THE RULE.
...

必勝
WHAT'S UP WITH THAT HAIR?!

IS THAT FOR OUR HIGH SCHOOL DEBUT?!
YOU GOT HORNS! JUST LIKE ME!
DARN RIGHT!
DON'T TOUCH 'EM, THOUGH!
NO REGRETS FOR ME. NOT ANYMORE.
I'M...GONNA BE A HERO WHO PROTECTS OTHERS.
SAY GOODBYE TO THE OLD, PATHETIC ME!!
...
KIRISHIMA. THAT DAY...
THAT REALLY HIT YOU HARD, HUH?
YEAH. SORRY.
YOU'RE STILL A BUNDLE OF NERVES!
WHAM
OW! THAT... DOESN'T HURT!!
BUT WHAT THE HECK?!
WHAM WHAM WHAM

OR ELSE I'LL START SPREADING RUMORS ABOUT *HIGH SCHOOL DEBUT MAN.*

It's gonna be fun.

HEH HEH HEH...

IF YOU OVERCOME THAT GLOOMY SELF OF YOURS...

...LET ME KNOW.

THE OLD YOU'S NOT GOING ANYWHERE WITH THAT EMO LOOK ON YOUR FACE!

THANKS.

AND THAT'S GOING BACK TO HOW I USED TO BE!!

BUT THERE'S ONE THING THAT SCARES ME MORE THAN ANYTHING...

I'VE CONFRONTED PLENTY OF SCARY STUFF SO FAR.

THAT'S WHY I NEVER WANNA REGRET ANYTHING EVER AGAIN!!

I'LL BE...
...A HERO WHO PROTECTS OTHERS.
YOU WANNA KNOW WHY YOU'RE GONNA LOSE?!
BECAUSE ALL OF US...
...INCLUDING ME...
...UNDER-ESTIMATED HIM!!
FWOOM
MAXIMUM DEFENSE!
NO USE.
SHSHK
GONNA CRACK.

THE HERO CALLED ...
... RED RIOT ...

...AND HIS CHIVAL-ROUS SPIRIT!

3rd

NO. 146 - TEMP SQUAD

MY HERO ACADEMIA

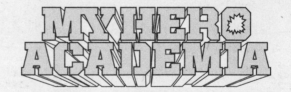

THIS SPEAR-AND-SHIELD BATTLE...
...IS OUR WIN!!
YOU OKAY, LITTLE BUD?!
WHOZZAT ...?
IT'S FAT! I TOOK CARE OF THE REST!
JUST TAKE A LOOK AROUND!

DO...WHAT I...CAN...

...GOTTA... I... PROTECT FAT...

KIRISHIMA

...

SPUNKY KIDS LIKE YOU ARE ALWAYS WELCOME HERE!

I SAW YOU AT THE SPORTS FESTIVAL!

FOR TAMAKI TO ACTUALLY BRING SOMEONE IN...

FAT GUM

...ABOUT HOW ENERGETIC KIDS ARE PERFECT FOR RAISING MORALE AT THE AGENCY...

FOURTH KIND SCOUTED ME FOR MY INTERNSHIP, AND HE SAID THE SAME THING...

CAN WE NOT TALK ABOUT ME...?

EVEN WITH HIS SKILLS, YOUR FRIEND THERE GETS NERVOUS AND RANKS SUPER LOW EVERY YEAR.

I WANNA BE LIKE THAT...!! THAT'S WHY I BUGGED TAMAKI SENPAI TO BRING ME HERE.

KLNCH

AND...I HATE THAT. CRIMSON RIOT WAS A HERO WHO REALLY PROTECTED PEOPLE...

BUT... THAT'S ALL I CAN DO...

YOU'VE DONE ENOUGH...! GOING THIS FAR, THOUGH...

BUT... NO MORE!

I'M JUST A PATHETIC GUY WHO ABANDONS PEOPLE IN DANGER.

THIS'S A DEATH MATCH... AND I...

...AIN'T DEAD YET!

SWISH

SWISH

NOT YET...

I'M ALL OUTTA FAT... AND RUNNING EMPTY ON STAMINA... WHAT DO WE DO?!

TMP

THIS SPEAR GUY'S CRAZY TOUGH! DID THE BARRIER MAN CUSHION THE BLOW SOMEHOW? EVEN SO...!!

!!

THERE'RE FIRST AID SUPPLIES DOWN THAT WAY.
PATCH THAT KID... NO, PATCH THAT *MAN* UP.
...
THIS IS A TRAP!
DO I LOOK LIKE THE CUNNING TYPE TO YOU?
RAPPA...!! STOP GOING OFF SCRIPT!!
CONTROLLING YOUR BATTLE-CRAZED LUNACY IS MY JOB!
YOU HAVE TO LISTEN TO ME!
HUH?
THINK ABOUT WHY THEY'D WANT A BRUTE LIKE YOU DOWN HERE! A BEAST WHO FEASTS ON VIOLENCE!!
WHAT ROLE ARE YOU MEANT TO PLAY, RAPPA?!

WHAM
YOU GOT NO ENERGY LEFT FOR BARRIERS, RIGHT?
THEN SHUT UP!
WHEEZE
I'M NOT DOING SO HOT MYSELF... I GOT THESE BROKEN BONES, AND I CAN'T EVEN LIFT MY ARMS.
WHAT'RE YOU REALLY AFTER?
A GOOD FIGHT. A DEATH MATCH.
YOU'VE HEARD OF UNDERGROUND FIGHTING RINGS, YEAH? CLUBS WHERE BRAWLERS BATTLE ALL OUT WITH QUIRKS.
NOT MANY HAVE STOOD BACK UP AFTER A BEATING FROM MY FISTS.
EVEN THOSE WHO DID WOULD ONLY BEG FOR THEIR LIVES.
Y'KNOW WHAT THAT'S LIKE? THE PAIN OF NEVER HAVING REAL SATISFACTION?!

ESPECIALLY RED-HAIR, THERE!!

I LIKE WHAT YOU GOT, KID!!

I DON'T KNOW WHY, BUT SOMETHING ABOUT PUTTING YOUR LIFE ON THE LINE IN BATTLE MAKES ME FEEL ALIVE...

I LOVE IT! YOU TWO ARE FREAKING GREAT!!

BETTER HEAL UP!! CUZ NEXT TIME WE FIGHT, YOU'RE A DEAD MAN!!

SO WE'RE GONNA HAVE A REMATCH TO THE DEATH!!

FAITHFUL TO HIS DESIRES... I DON'T SENSE ANY DISHONESTY FROM HIM.

I GUESS THAT'S THE WAY A WEIRDO LIKE HIM THINKS...

EITHER WAY, REJOINING THE GROUP'S GONNA BE TOUGH IN THIS STATE...

A DRAW? IS THIS YOUR SENSE OF SPORTS-MANSHIP?

GIMME A BREAK! NO ONE'S DEAD, SO THIS IS A DRAW!!

WOMP

WOMP

GET IT? THERE AIN'T GONNA BE A NEXT TIME. YOU LOST!

BUT YOU'LL BE ARRESTED AND LOCKED UP SOON ENOUGH!

...WHAT IT'S LIKE TO KNOW YOUR OWN WEAKNESSES.

BUT TAMAKI BROUGHT YOU OVER CUZ HE UNDER- STANDS...

YOU CAME TO ME FEELING SO PATHETIC... SO HOPELESS... I COULD SEE THAT.

KIRISHIMA...

SHF

THAT MAN!

GOOO

I CAN'T WAIT TO DESTROY HIM AGAIN!

EVEN THE ENEMY RECOGNIZES YOU.

MORE THAN A HERO...

AND NOW LOOK.

YOU SHOWED YOURSELF HOW THERE'S NOTHING PATHETIC ABOUT YOU.

THAT SHOULD STOP THE BLEEDING FOR NOW, ANYWAY.
I KNOW YOU AIN'T GONNA LIKE IT, BUT YOU GOTTA REST HERE FOR A WHILE.
ALL HEALED UP? CAN I KILL HIM?
NOT YET! LET THE KID BREATHE A LITTLE!
...
SINCE YOU'RE IN SUCH A SHARING MOOD...
WELL, THIS MIGHT BE WEIRD FOR A HERO TO ASK, BUT...
RAPPA... WHY'RE YOU RUNNING WITH THIS SMALL-TIME GANG?

LOST TO...?

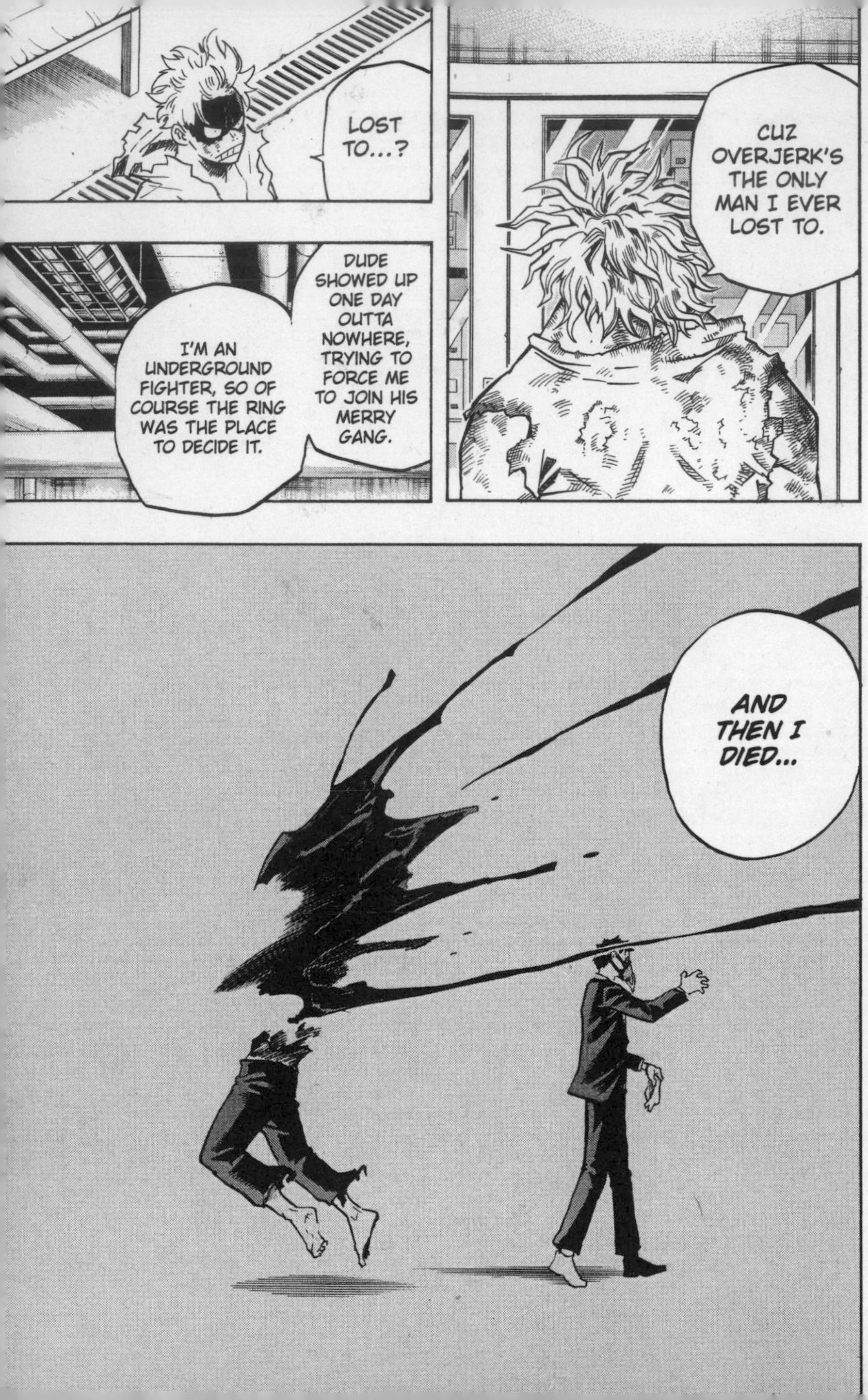

CUZ OVERJERK'S THE ONLY MAN I EVER LOST TO.

I'M AN UNDERGROUND FIGHTER, SO OF COURSE THE RING WAS THE PLACE TO DECIDE IT.

DUDE SHOWED UP ONE DAY OUTTA NOWHERE, TRYING TO FORCE ME TO JOIN HIS MERRY GANG.

AND THEN I DIED...

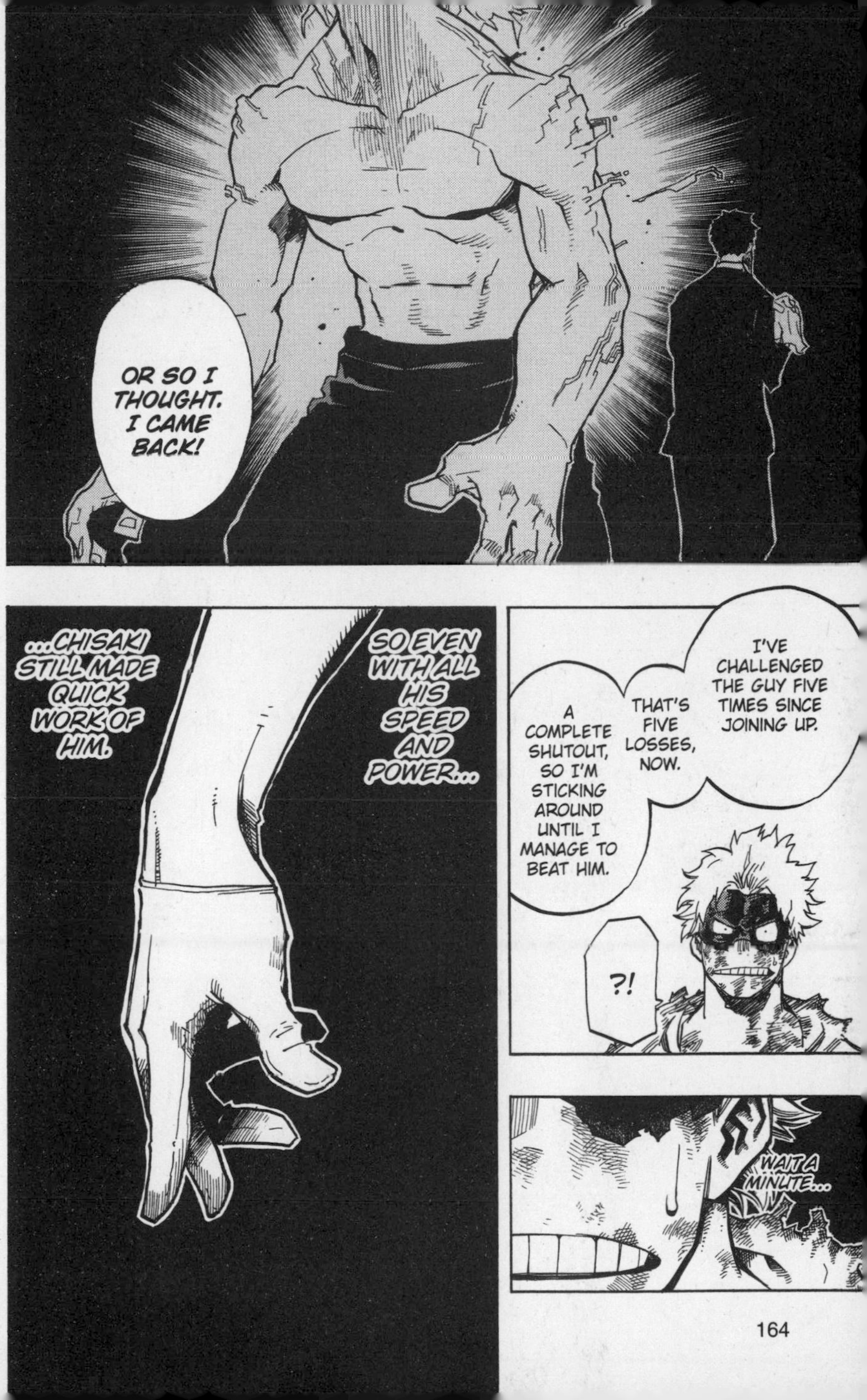
OR SO I THOUGHT. I CAME BACK!
SO EVEN WITH ALL HIS SPEED AND POWER...
...CHISAKI STILL MADE QUICK WORK OF HIM.
I'VE CHALLENGED THE GUY FIVE TIMES SINCE JOINING UP.
THAT'S FIVE LOSSES, NOW.
A COMPLETE SHUTOUT, SO I'M STICKING AROUND UNTIL I MANAGE TO BEAT HIM.
?!
WAIT A MINUTE...

WHY'S THE BIG GUY NOT MAKING A SHOWING HIMSELF?

THAT JERK! HE'S JUST RUNNING AND HIDING!

HE'S CRAZY STRONG BUT LEAVES THE FIGHTING TO HIS LACKEYS...

WHAT'S CHISAKI TRYING TO DO?

BRING THE YAKUZA BACK TO POWER!

SO COCKY. YOU THINK WE, THE ENEMY, WOULD EVER—

BUT HE NEEDS A TON OF CASH TO MAKE IT HAPPEN. ONCE HE'S GOT THAT...

STOP!!

RAPPA!!

CAN'T SAY I KNOW THE DETAILS, BUT I'VE HEARD SOME THINGS.

HE'S GONNA DISTRIBUTE A HUGE LOAD OF SOMETHING OR OTHER...

THE DAY IT ALL GOES DOWN WON'T BE FAR OFF!

TURNING BACK THE CLOCK... UNDERGROUND, JUST AFTER THE INITIAL ASSAULT...
WHAT A RACKET...
THEY'D BETTER BE DOING THEIR JOBS...
HATE TO SAY IT, BUT...
THE HASSAIKAI IS FINISHED.
MOST OF THE MEN ARE IN THE BOSS'S CAMP AND NOT EXACTLY DOWN WITH MY WAY OF THINKING.
EVEN THOUGH I RESPECT THE BOSS'S WILL MORE THAN ANY OF THEM.
AS LONG AS THE BOSS AND I STILL LIVE, THE HASSAIKAI CAN'T DIE.
WITH JUST THE *FINISHED PRODUCT*...
...AND THE *SERUM*...
I CAN BRING ABOUT OUR REVIVAL.
AND THIS WHOLE NASTY BUSINESS IS JUST THE THING OUR FRIENDS WITH VESTED INTERESTS ENJOY.
THEY'LL LOVE THE IDEA OF A DRUG THAT SCARES HEROES AND WILL HAPPILY INVEST.
WHOOSH

ON THAT NOTE...
TIME TO EARN YOUR KEEP, TEMP SQUAD.

OKAAAY ...
LEAVE IT TO US, OVER-HAUL!

I DIDN'T EXPLAIN THIS IN THE STORY, BUT RAPPA'S QUIRK IS *STRONGARM*. HIS SHOULDERS CAN ROTATE INSANELY QUICK, ALLOWING HIM TO WHIP OUT A FIERCE BARRAGE OF PUNCHES.

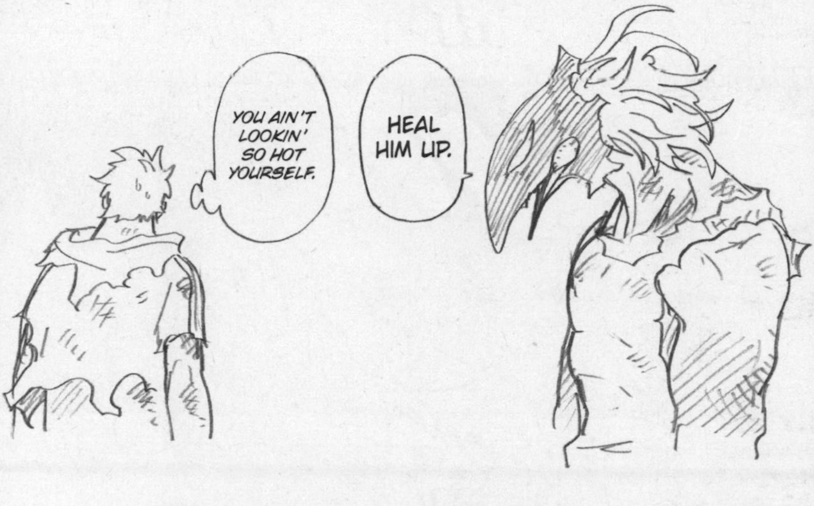

DRAWING RAPPA IS A LOT OF FUN.

DOES THIS GUY EVER LET UP?!

HERE IT COMES AGAIN!!

BACK TO THE PRESENT WITH TEAM NIGHTEYE!!

EVEN THE FLOOR!!

THE WALLS!!

THE CEILING!!

NO.147 - TWOGA!!

WE'RE GONNA GET GROUND INTO HAMBURGERS!!

HE'S TRYING TO CRUSH US TO DEATH!!

...!

HASSAIKAI DIRECTOR IRINAKA IS USING THE WALLS TO SLOW EVERYONE DOWN!

YOU REALLY SCREWED UP, HERE!!

SOME LEADER YOU ARE, GETTING US INTO THIS MESS!

BAM

ROCK LOCK!!

...GETS COMPLETELY LOCKED IN PLACE!

KRIM

KRIK

OVER HERE!

HE AIN'T SHIFTING THIS PART FOR NOW!

DEAD-BOLT!!

TWIST

SHFFF

ANYTHING I LOCK DOWN!...

KRIK

ANYTHING HE TOUCHES (BESIDES LIVING THINGS) GETS LOCKED IN PLACE!! BUT HE'S GOT HIS LIMITS WHEN IT COMES TO LOCKING DOWN POWERFUL FORCES OR WIDE AREAS!

THIS IS THE LIMIT OF MY RANGE!

AT MAXIMALIM SECURITY LEVEL, MY LOCK DOWN CAN'T COVER TOO MANY SPOTS AT ONCE.

AND DON'T COMPLAIN ABOUT THE TIGHT QUARTERS.

LOCK HERO ROCK LOCK

QUIRK: LOCK DOWN!!

WATCH OUT!!

SHFFFA

HE'S COMING FROM THE SPOTS I CAN'T PIN DOWN! LOOK!

HUFF!

HUFF!

HE'S LIKE SOME SORT OF WHACKED-OUT MOLE.

HE'S PROBABLY BURROWING THROUGH THE SHIFTING WALLS, FOCUSING ON ONE SPOT AT A TIME.

WE AIN'T MAKING ANY HEADWAY, HERE! WE JUST KEEP GETTING CORNERED!

SHF SHF

THAT'S WHY HE'S TARGETING ME WITH HIS ATTACK.

I ONLY NEED TO SPOT HIS REAL BODY TO STOP HIM!

HE MUST BE WATCHING US FROM SOMEWHERE! SOMEWHERE IN THESE WALLS...

I KNOW!

ERASER!

THINGS WOULD BE GOING A LOT SMOOTHER IF TEAM FAT WAS HERE.

BUT IRINAKA IS GETTING BACKED INTO A CORNER TOO!

TO MAKE IT HAPPEN, HE'D HAVE TO BEAT A TEAM OF SKILLED HEROES IN A CONTEST OF SPEED.

THE REASON HE DIDN'T TRY THIS STIFLING STRATEGY FROM THE VERY START...

...IS BECAUSE MANIPULATING A HUGE MASS AT HIGH SPEED REQUIRES AN EQUALLY IMPRESSIVE AMOUNT OF STAMINA.

BUT USING QUIRK BOOSTERS TO POWER UP TAKES A TOLL ON IRINAKA, LEAVING HIM UNABLE TO BLOCK THEIR PROGRESS!

HASSAIKAI DIRECTOR
MIMIC (JOI IRINAKA)

DESPITE BEING SLOWED DOWN, HE'S BEEN THROWN INTO A PANIC BY THE FACT THAT THE INVADERS ARE PUSHING AHEAD.

I CAN'T LET 'EM GET THROUGH...

AND NOW HE'S STARTED WITH THIS CRUSHING PLAN...

...BECAUSE THE DRUGS HE TOOK ARE ABOUT TO WEAR OFF.

THAT VULNERABILITY FORCED HIM TO BE CAUTIOUS.

BUT IT'S THAT VERY CAUTION THAT ALLOWED HIM TO BECOME THE FACILITY'S DIRECTOR.

CAN'T LET THEM...!!
WE'VE ALREADY CHOSEN TO TAKE THE LOW ROAD!!
KRIK
KRIK
NO SENSE IN HOLDING BACK NOW!!
HUFF!
HUFF!
WE'RE NOT GETTING ANYWHERE!!
KRIK
!
"THERE'S A CHILD IN NEED OUT THERE. THAT'S WHAT MATTERS MOST."
RYUKYU AND THE GIRLS...
THE HEROES... ALL THE POLICE, HERE!
DON'T GO...
KIRISHIMA AND FAT GUM!
THEY ALL GOT US THIS FAR!
NO WAY YOU'RE STOPPING US!!

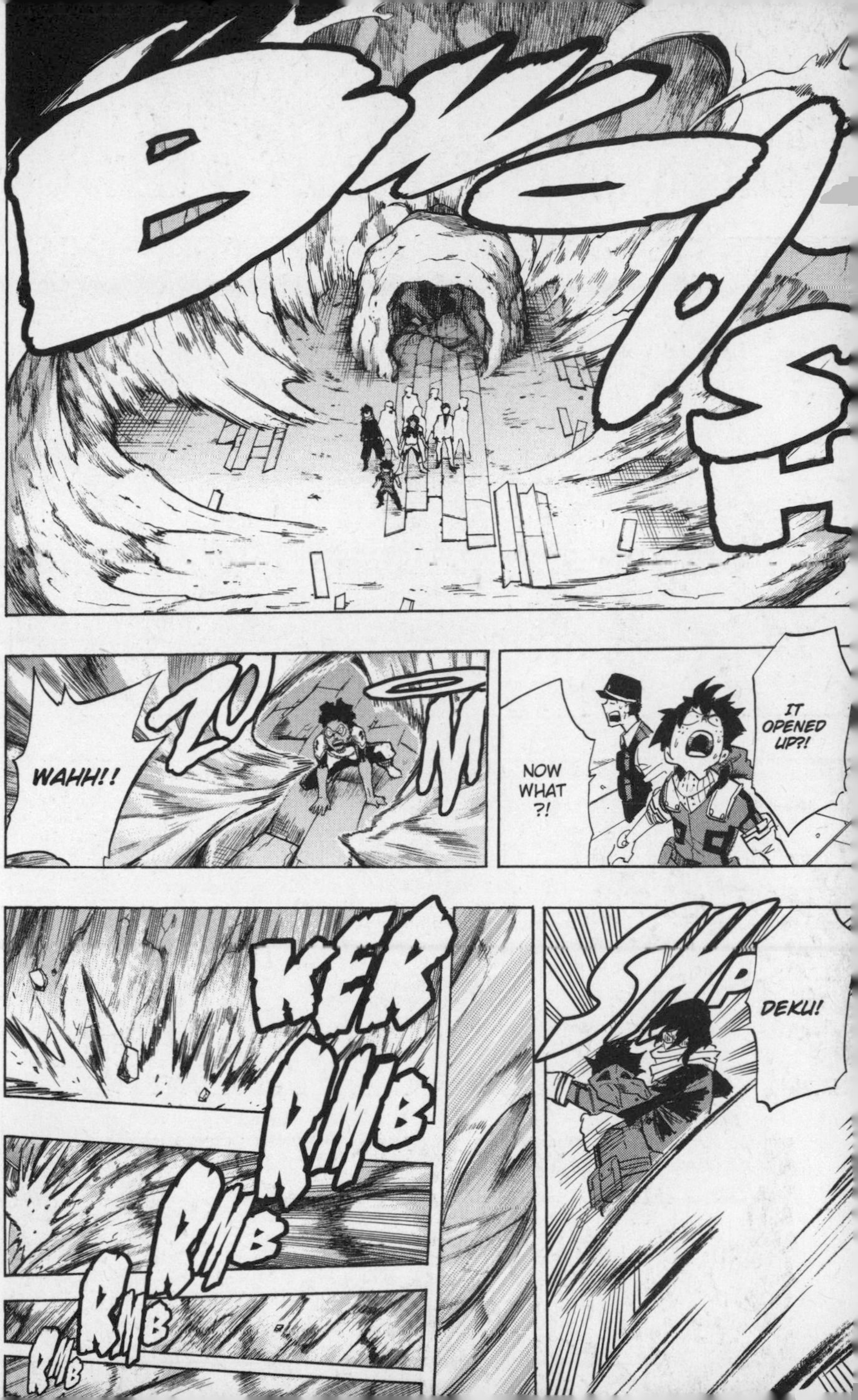

WAHH!!

NOW WHAT ?!

IT OPENED UP?!

DEKU!

WHOOSH
WE GOT SPLIT UP?!
NOT AGAIN...
No worries.
Thanks for that.
HEY!! YOU GUYS STILL ALIVE?!
THAT'S ROCK LOCK'S VOICE!!
THE WALL CAN'T BE THAT THICK, THEN...
DID HE CHANGE TACTICS SINCE HE COULDN'T CRUSH US?
IT SEEMS LIKE IT'S EASIER FOR US TO MOVE NOW...
THERE MUST BE SOMETHING ELSE GOING ON HERE...
SOME-THING'S COMING!!
SHADDUP. IT'S YOUR FAULT, AIN'T IT...?
THEIR NEXT MOVE!!
SHAH

SHK
WHO'S THIS?!

STUPID
LEAGUE
OF V–

HUH
?!

K·SH ING

LOCK
DOWN
!!

SPLOOSH

SHH!

SHP

TOGA THE
YAKUZA..

A REAL
NASTY
GANGSTER.

YOU'RE
WRONG. I'M
NOW A
PROTECTED
TREASURE
FROM A
GOLDEN ERA.

NK

ROCK!! WHAT'S GOING ON?!
ERASER! STAND ASIDE!
ROCK LOCK!
BAM
THIS IMPOSTOR JUST SHOWED UP AND CAME AT ME!
WATCH OUT! THERE COULD BE MORE REINFORCE-MENTS SOMEWHERE!!
A BLADE WOUND...?!

YOU OKAY, MIDORIYA?
YEAH! LET'S HURRY UP AND GET CHISAKI...
LOOM
GAH!
IMPOSTOR.
BLADE WOUND.
WE DIDN'T THINK THESE GUYS FOUND COMMON GROUND WITH THE LEAGUE.
WE WERE WRONG !!

BU
RST
HIMIKO TOGA ?!
TOGA!! YES, IT'S ME, TOGA! YOU REMEMBERED !!
I'M SO VERY GLAD TO SEE YOU AGAIN!!
STUMBL
I COULD NOT BE HAP-PIER, IZUKU !!

SO, SO THRILLED !!
ACTUALLY... THIS GIVES US THE CHANCE TO STOP THEM HERE AS WELL!
THAT'S FAR ENOUGH, HIMIKO TOGA!
SHP

FWIP
SHUK!
ROLL ROLL ROLL
FLAP
WHUFF
SENSEI ?!

I'M FINE. STAY BACK!
SHF SHF
!!
SLAM
THE TWO GANGS ARE WORKING TOGETHER...
MAYBE THE STRATEGY CHANGED SO SUDDENLY BECAUSE THE LEAGUE HAS JOINED?
HAHH...
HAHH...
I'M SO GLAD I GOT TRANS-FERRED HERE...
EVER PLAY SHOGI?

DON'T BE LIKE THAT.

THIS IS YOUR CHANCE TO PICK UP A NEW HOBBY.

HEY, LET'S PLAY!!

NAH, SO PUT IT AWAY. I DON'T EVEN KNOW THE RULES.

...IS HOW YOU CAN UTILIZE PIECES STOLEN FROM THE OPPONENT.

MY FAVORITE PART ABOUT SHOGI...

YOU LEARN HOW TO STEP BACK AND TAKE STOCK OF THE WHOLE GAME.

HM...

I CAN'T FEEL AT EASE WITH THEM RUNNING AMOK.

SO GIVE ME KUROGIRI OR TOGA. PERHAPS BUBAIGAWARA.

I DIVULGED EVERY LAST DETAIL OF MY GRAND PLAN.

TO BUILD TRUST BETWEEN US...

SO NOW IT'S YOUR TURN TO DO ME A SOLID.

...AND HELP CLEAR AWAY THE ILL WILL.

THEY'RE MY CORNERSTONES!! WHY DO YOU WANT 'EM SO BAD?

THEY ALL HAVE THEIR USES... YOU TRYING TO SLOW DOWN MY OPERATION?

SKRGH

YOU'RE ALL ABOUT...
...MAKING FRIENDS, RIGHT?
SO SAD ABOUT THIS, SHIGARAKI...
BUT I'M REALLY PUMPED!!
VOLUME 16 - RED RIOT (END)

THE GRUDGE

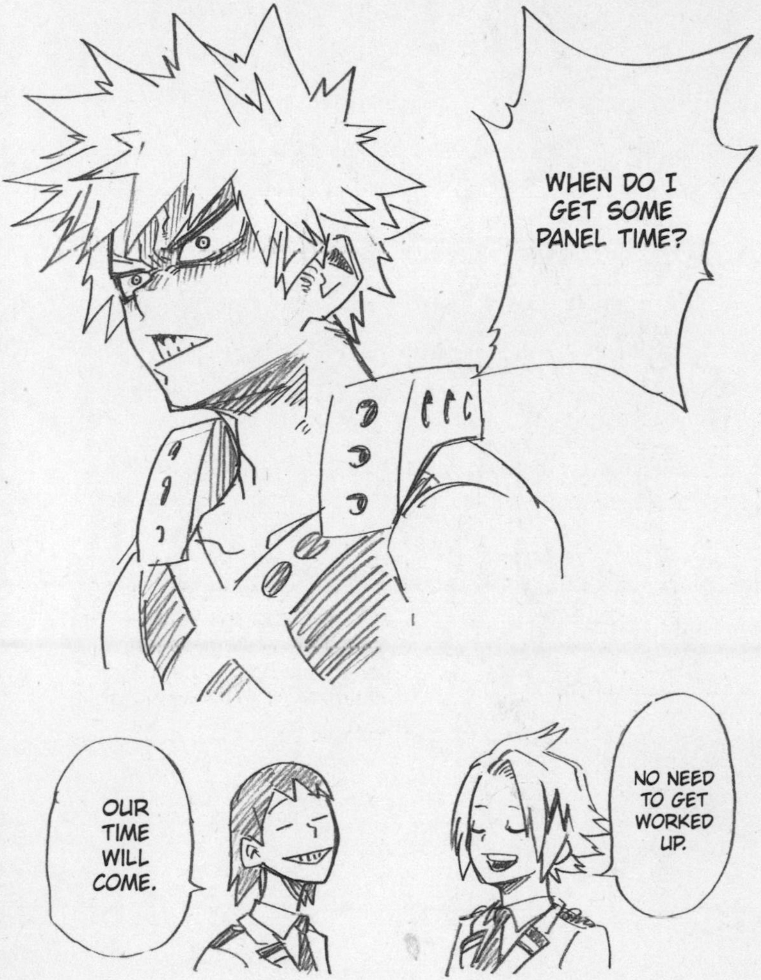

An early sketch of Eri. Went into the scrap pile because she looks a little ***too*** ready for action. She's a hard character, in more ways than one.

IKEDA-KUN
HATER
Everyone presented these to me out of the blue, so I had to showcase them here! All so cool!! I wanna use them in the story!!
YUZAWA-SAN
VAN BANSHEE
IRONISH MAN
FUJIYA-KUN

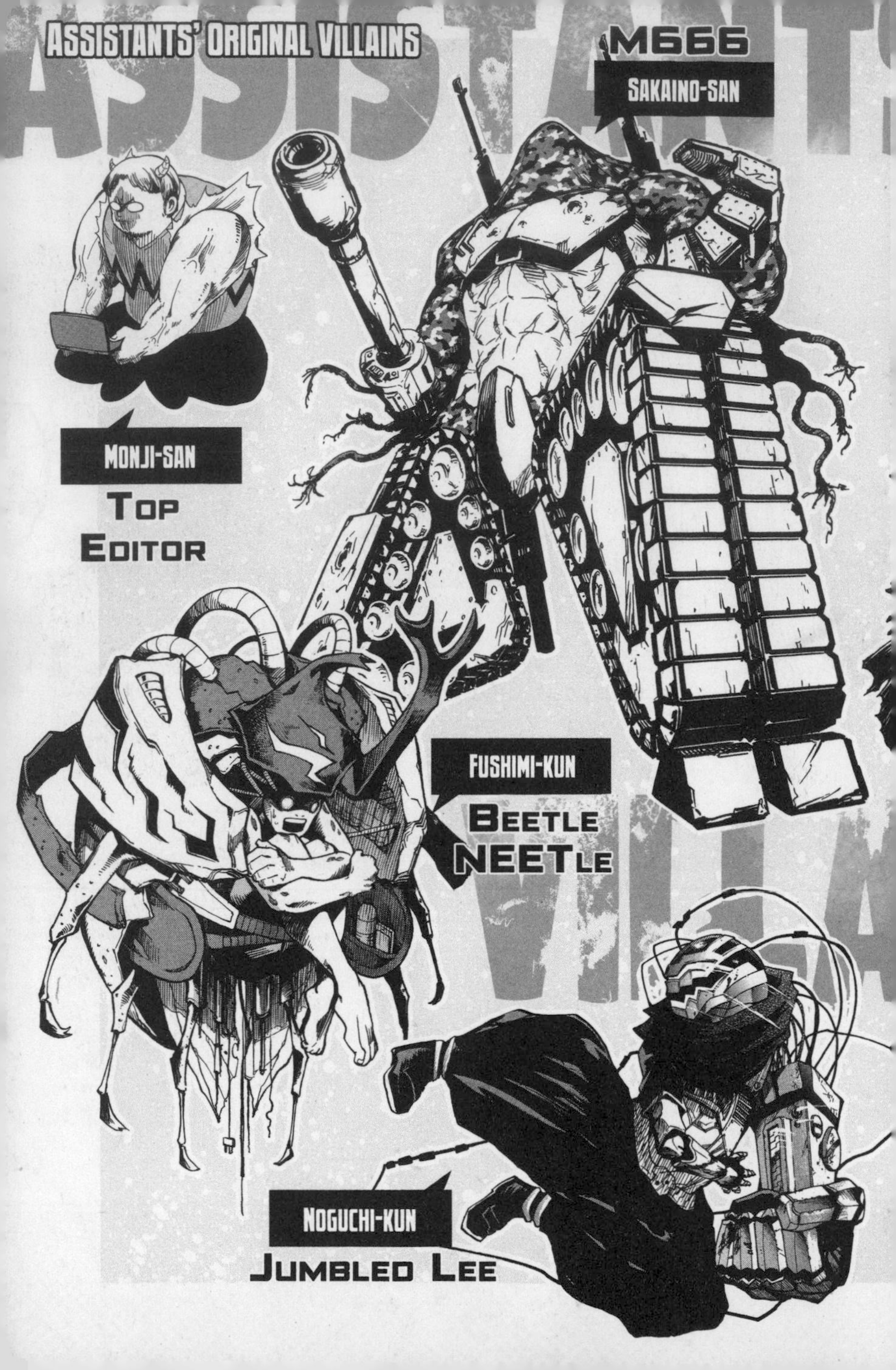
ASSISTANTS' ORIGINAL VILLAINS
M666
SAKAINO-SAN
MONJI-SAN
TOP EDITOR
FUSHIMI-KUN
BEETLE NEETLE
NOGUCHI-KUN
JUMBLED LEE

MY HERO ACADEMIA

reads from right to left, starting in the upper-right corner. Japanese is read from right to left, meaning that action, sound effects and word-balloon order are completely reversed from English order.

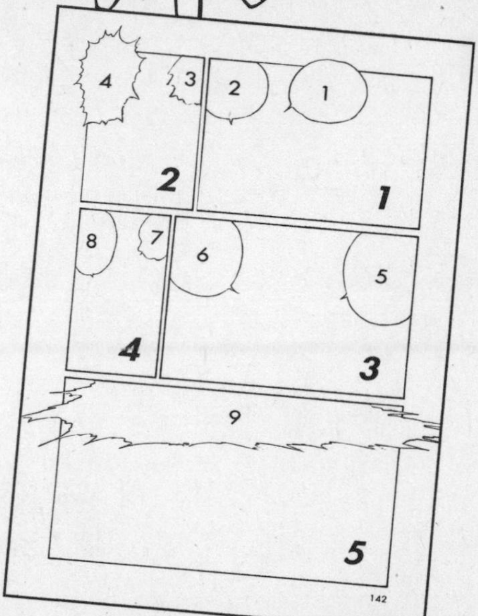